The Essential Guide for

New Project managers

How to overcome common Project Management Challenges

Bonus IT Project Management Course including 20+ Professional
Templates & Checklists

Yassine Tounsi

Preface

Project management challenges frequently arise as questions, and most project management questions have the same answer: "It depends." Taking into consideration that each project is unique, no specific solution for a given problem is likely to work for all projects and situations. That said, there are key principles and practices that prove to be effective.

For many of the project management challenges included in this book, the discussion begins with some qualifications describing the response, including factors to consider when dealing with the issue at hand.

This book is based on questions I have been asked throughout my career as a project manager. The suggested solutions are not on theoretical matters, the focus of this guide is on real problems encountered by both novice and experienced project managers, trying to get their projects done in today's stress-filled environment.

However, keep in mind that your judgment is essential to solving your particular problem. Consider your specific circumstances and strive to "make the punishment fit the crime." Adapt the solutions offered in this guide if they appear helpful and disregard them if the advice seems irrelevant to your own situation.

My initial advice would be to confront issues and problems early when they are tractable and can be resolved with the least effort and the fewest interventions. Escalate as a last resort, but never hesitate to do so when it is necessary. Good relationships and trust are key to efficient problem resolution, and they are built by treating people the way you want to be treated, so act accordingly.

Given the broad spectrum of project types and situations, it's unlikely that any book will cover all possible issues and scenarios and their solutions. Nonetheless, I hope that this guide will help you successfully launch your career as a Project Manager, ace your first project, and handle whatever challenge you're going to face while retaining your sanity in the process.

Good Luck!

Introduction

When thinking about this book's introduction, I thought it would be suitable to tell you about the story of how Microsoft officially came up with the Project Manager position in the late 80s. However, when I reflected on it, project management started way back before even Microsoft thought to create a formal role for it within its multinational corporation's structure.

Contemplating some of humanity's creations such as the Pyramids of Giza, the hanging gardens of Babylon, the Great Wall of China, or the Coliseum, I think we can all agree that project management is an ancient practice. Long before project management was structured and guided by experts and books, humans were able to conduct several colossal projects with unbelievable success.

These project examples prove that Project management has been practiced for as long as humanity inhabited earth; we played the role of project managers without being aware of it, through creating an environment for people to work together, achieve a mutual objective, and eventually deliver successful projects, despite all the primitive tools, hard conditions, and various complexities and uncertainties. Unfortunately, the methods and techniques used to carry out many of these monumental achievements were not documented, even though they had an enormous workforce, large scope, years of work, advanced planning, and precise execution.

Throughout history, the ingenious architects and engineers that delivered the aforementioned impressive projects were serving their primary roles of specialty as well as being project managers. They had to manage hundreds to thousands of workers for many years, ensure there was enough supply to sustain the project, make sure the project was on track, and of course, the end result had to fulfill the expectations of their commanders. This manifests that, contrary to what many might think, history is filled with many projects that had project sponsorship, project management team, practiced project processes, and basic understanding of the principle project phases.

In 1950, organizations started implementing structured and systematic tools and techniques to execute complex projects such as the Manhattan Project that produced the first nuclear weapons. The 1960s witnessed ambitious projects such as landing a man on the moon which utilized tools for managing large scope projects. In the 1970s, project management software started to see light due to technological advancement.

1980 brought affordable PCs, and subsequently smaller companies started to use computers for project management. Here comes the suitable placement in this historical sequencing for Microsoft's story that I was intending to narrate in my introduction; in the late 1980s, Microsoft was about to embark on a large-scale project when they faced a problem: there were far too many parties engaged. No one knew how to organize all of the marketing, engineering, and business end teams.

So, Microsoft devised what ended up to be an excellent solution: They assigned one person with the significant responsibility to arrange and coordinate their new project. Everything proceeded smoothly after Microsoft designated a dedicated leader, and the teams were way more satisfied with their work dynamics. Excel was the eventual outcome of this new work method. And ultimately, Microsoft made this new role a staple for all their projects. Thus, the Project Manager position was officially born.

Project management kept evolving with the appearance of project management degrees, institutions, and certifications. Moreover, project management theories, tools, and techniques started to become mainstream in many organizations and industries. Projects in the next era were illustrated by the application of high technology. Technology continued to be a driving force for change and greatly impacted what project managers were doing. In 2001, project management took another revolutionary step with The Agile Manifesto being written and introduced to practitioners. With the ongoing standardization of processes, refinement of concepts, and development of software and applications, project management became more of a science than art.

As there was no consensus on the specific beginning of project management in history, it seems that there is no consensus on the future of project management too; Some experts think that project management will be a required work skill for all positions and specialties, while others argue that all industries have a need for unique profiles with specialized training and credentials in project management.

According to the PMI's "Job growth and Talent gap in Project management" report, there'll be a need of filling breakthrough 87.7 million PM roles by 2027, and that the annualized median salary of a PM Professional in the USA will reach 120K US Dollars. Both perspectives agree on the necessity of having what it takes to successfully manage a project in today's work market.

Moreover, as the dynamics and environment of organizations evolve, the challenges for future project managers will follow suit. With large complex projects, it's becoming a necessity for the project manager to be able to coordinate multi-disciplinary knowledge and effectively adapt to new technologies and learn which specialized intricate tools will work best for each project. Another challenge for project managers will be cutting through the ceaseless sea of information by filtering abundant data and capturing the right information. Understanding the big picture and effectively communicating with others, having to work across networks, with people in different countries, and people who come from different cultures will only compound the complexities for future project managers. Project managers will also have to adapt to shifting organizational structure, limited resources, stakeholders, competition, economics, and many other factors that are contributing to the transformation of organizations and business environments.

All of these challenges that project managers, especially the novice ones, are fated to tackle, are what ignited this book's idea. This content was created with the purpose of guiding ambitious new Project managers to succeed in their first projects, as it might be a shaping factor that will affect their whole career path. This book was created to help you navigate through common challenges and issues, be adaptable to constant change, uncertainty, and disruptions, and advancements in technology, acquire the needed set of skills, and learn new specialized skills, ultimately covering the fundamental elements that make a project manager a great one; leadership, decisiveness, communication, and foresight to name a few.

We're going to focus on five main areas: Career, Business challenges, Communication & Leadership, Technical skills, and finally Agile, to cover common challenges project managers face through their debut in this position.

Under the Career section, we're going to explain what is the proper way to get into such a role and what a Project Manager position concretely involves. In the Business challenges part, we're going to help you address your upper management's inquiries and requests, as well as guiding you through the common issues you might face while practicing your role. The Communication & Leadership section will identify key practices in order to efficiently communicate and be the leader you aspire to be. Throughout the Technical skills section, we're going to grant you some foundational knowledge on how to effectively and practically manage your project. Finally, under the Agile part of this course, we will be clarifying the main aspects of this approach and its implementation.

If this sounds like what you're looking for to step up into your first project with the needed self-confidence and understanding of what you're going to face, let's not waste time and get down to business!

PS: To access the bonus IT Project Management course included with this book and the 20+ Professional templates and checklists it comprises, you will find at the end of the book the link to get it for free.

I. Career

According to a Project Management Institute report, "Demand over the next 10 years for project managers is growing faster than demand for workers in other occupations".

Apart from the increase of project management positions in the future, PM jobs will be also financially rewarding. As per the same report, the salaries of project management-oriented professionals in projectized sectors are 82% higher than those of non-project-oriented professionals.

Consequently, a lot of job seekers are considering going through this career path. But, as appealing as it may appear, this position is not made for everyone.

Building a successful career as a project manager doesn't happen overnight: it requires a certain type of personality, an exceptional set of both technical and soft skills, and a consistent amount of hard work.

In the first section of this book, we are discussing in detail the project manager job requirements, along with the first steps to take to launch a successful career.

Let's get started with the first challenge!

How to get into a project management role?

Short Answer

To get into a project manager role, you need both knowledge and experience. Knowledge can be acquired through a university degree, certifications, online courses, books, etc. Also, working as a member of a project will help you to acquire and develop a set of soft skills and expertise in your field which will eventually qualify you to step in as a project manager.

Explanation

To become a project manager, you must have both an educational background and experience in order to master the basics of project management. Beyond the formal training, you also need analytical skills, communication skills, leadership, and even guts, as this field is methodical and scrupulous.

1. How you could learn about project management

Online training might be the most obvious way to acquire project management knowledge. A structured or formal training, like a certification course, can be a huge asset along with affordable online courses that can be found on platforms such as Udemy, LinkedIn Learning, Coursera, Edx, etc.

Some organizations have internal programs that help you transition to project management, or they might equally provide coaching and mentoring opportunities. If your company offers project management training, you should take advantage of it.

You can always reach out to an experienced project manager for mentoring and guidance. For beginners, a mentor can represent a trusted ally and a valuable source of knowledge as well, due to their experience in the field. Along with guidance, mentors can provide you with constructive criticism which will help you see things from an unbiased, new perspective, leading you eventually to further develop yourself, navigate landmines, and work through unspoken rules. It's important to have at least one mentor who is doing the job you're aspiring to land, as they can help you discover and learn what this position is about before even getting into it. Don't underestimate the value of having a mentor by your side: These connections often pave your way for success.

If you happen to be incapable of finding someone to play your mentor's role, you can consider getting some books treating project management fundamentals, such as this guide, to go through the basics. You can look for "Tool Kits" or "for Dummies" books to get you familiar with the role's foundational responsibilities, skills, and practices. Amazon should be your go-to place for purchasing books as it provides a wide selection of Kindle, print, and even audiobooks.

2. What kind of experience you should have

There are numerous job titles, from entry to executive-level, that you should consider as you work your way up to the project manager position.

Regardless of the field, an aspiring project manager might start their career path as a Project Coordinator, Project Scheduler, Assistant Project Manager, Business analyst, Technical manager, Programmer, Engineer, Management support specialist, etc.

Aside from getting a college education related to your field, the experience that such roles offer can help you gain the necessary project management skills to make you an eligible candidate for the position. After which, you can either get promoted to project manager at your current organization or you could apply for the job at another company.

When it comes to building your project management skills, work experience can be the best way to gain a combination of hard skills, like planning and risk management, as well as soft skills such as communication and the ability to motivate your team.

Developing a skill set of technical, analytical, communication and leadership skills is a must for this position. Being a project manager will require you to know how to communicate with your team effectively. Good communication skills will not just help you delegate tasks to your team, but it will also allow you to disseminate confidence and trust among project stakeholders.

There are many professionals who seem to innately have skills like leadership, time management, and critical thinking. If you feel that you may be lacking in some particular areas, such as budgeting or scheduling, don't worry!

Continuously working on developing and acquiring the required skills will make you prepared once the opportunity comes up.

If you lack experience, however, volunteering, internships, part-time or summer jobs, and any other activity that includes personal interaction, teamwork, and mainly any type of responsibility can be key to developing your character and especially your communication and leadership potential.

***

While the qualities mentioned above are always part of what companies look for in project managers, you should keep in mind that criteria frequently vary, as they initially depend on the organization you are intending to apply to, as well as the industry in which the company operates. For instance, an IT company may require experience with Agile projects, while a construction company may ask for experience with Engineering, Procurement, and Construction (EPC) projects.

Do you need a certificate in project management?

Short Answer

People are divided concerning this matter into pro-certification and anti-certification: One camp considers that certifications can form a stepping stone for your career. Others consider that certifications have no value since certifying organizations are mainly looking for profit. I personally stand in the middle: certificates are not the standard of whether or not you are a successful project manager, but you may need one to achieve progress since they present some sort of knowledge approval.

Explanation

Whether to choose to pursue a project management certification or an academic degree, fully depends on your age and background, as well as your current or target future field and discipline. Let's go through the two options in detail.

1. When you don't need certification

Professionals who are not completely sure about pursuing a career in project management may consider certification as a heavy upfront investment. Not getting a certification until practicing the job for a while and verifying whether it fits your profile or not is a sound choice.

The cost and effort of getting certified in project management may not be worthwhile for project managers who are not intending to switch to other companies. Yet, in order to keep their knowledge up to date, they attend seminars or webinars, read blog articles and books, or take part in online or onsite courses.

Another reason for experienced PMs to not pursue certifications is that they usually consider project management as a transitioning phase to later move on to executive positions like Chief executive officer (CEO) or Chief Technical Officer (CTO).

Even Though, certificates could improve their resume, in most cases, not having one is not considered as an impediment to achieving their ambitions.

Likewise, not all aspiring entrepreneurs see the value of being certified. Nevertheless, they may encourage their team members to get certified in order to apply project management practices in a more methodical way within their startup.

2. When do you need certification?

For people who are just starting their professional careers, or who aspire to make a move into project management, seeking a project management certificate is often a good decision.

Some forms of project management certifications are increasingly encouraged or even required for many positions in project management. The Project Management Professional (PMP) certification is usually the most common choice for those with project management experience. However, with less to no experience, CAMP would be the most adequate option.

Such certifications may help particularly those who want to move into project management or wish to transition into a new field. Certification can add value to your resume, especially that nowadays project management jobs are high in demand. In many cases, a certification proves to be beneficial as some companies use it as a basis to shortlist candidates. Many companies even consider a project management certification to be mandatory as you may not be eligible to apply for certain positions without the required credentials.

A Project Management certification is also highly useful if you want to step up your career at your current organization. It puts you ahead of your colleagues in terms of moving up the career ladder. For instance, a certified manager can do much better than a non-certified one in a grueling project management interview.

Increasingly, clients of most of the big companies tend to demand that their projects are managed by certified PMs. In such a situation, certification gives you the leverage and chance to be the one to handle prestigious clients. A project management certification is a proof that you possess the knowledge and expertise that match a Project Manager's position prerequisites. Plus, your capabilities as a certified project manager will enable you to contribute to your organization's success. This is why the majority of organizations are setting project management certificates as an important criterion nowadays.

***

Obtaining a project management credential depends on your career aspirations and the industry you work in. Such a credential is useful if you work in an industry with a lot of bureaucracy. In small companies, on the other hand, a certificate can be pointless as your knowledge will not be applicable to the types of projects they conduct.

A project management certificate is not a magic tool that will turn you into an exceptional project manager. It's merely an indication that you are proficient with the fundamentals of project management.

Some people might view certifications as costly, time-consuming, and laborious. However, many recruiting experts consider project management certificates as a valuable credential that adds credibility to your resume and proves you possess the necessary skills to excel in your position. So yes, certifications are in most cases worth the effort, especially if you want to advance your career, if your organization uses some project management framework, or if you want to better manage projects.

What are the most common project management certifications?

Short Answer

Beginners can go for a Certified Associate in Project Management (CAPM) certificate. But the most recognized certifications when going through job offers are Project Management Professional (PMP) and PRojects IN Controlled Environments (Prince2).

PMP and Prince2 embrace the Agile methodology which is widely implemented especially in the IT sector. However, further specialized certificates in Agile are arising, such as Certified Scrum Master (CSM) and Professional Scrum Master (PSM).

Besides the ones mentioned above, you can opt for many other project management certificates depending on your preferences and requirements.

Explanation

Before you start on the career path of a Project Manager, you might need to complete some formal education or training. Many universities offer undergraduate, Bachelor's, or Master's degrees specialized in project management. Yet, enrolling in a certification program can be a better option if you already have some level of understanding and knowledge of project management principles acquired through previous studies or work experience.

The right project management certificate program can help you accelerate your professional career by honing your leadership and tactical skills and boosting your visibility to senior executives. Choosing a confirmed and reliable provider for your project management training is a crucial step towards achieving your objective. A project management certification is an excellent career move, but it's important to assess the benefits and drawbacks of common certification programs before diving in.

1. Project Management Professional (PMP)

The Project Management Institute (PMI) calls its internationally recognized certification "the gold standard of project management." The PMI does not endorse any particular resources or materials for the PMP certification preparation. However, they do recommend a reference list of ten resources including their Project Management Body of Knowledge (PMBOK) and the Agile practice guide.

There are two options to qualify for the PMP certification exam, both require 35 hours of education (also known as contact hours)[1]. For the first option, a four-year degree is necessary, along with a minimum of 4,500 hours of work experience (approximately two and a half years of a full-time job) as well as the required 35 contact hours. The second way involves a mandatory 35 contact hours too plus a secondary degree, and 7,500 hours of work experience (about four years of a full-time job).

The exam comprises 180 questions with a duration of 230 minutes, focusing on three main domains: People, Process, and Business environment. Predictive, agile, and hybrid approaches are included across the three exam domains[2].

A PMP certificate requires renewal every three years[3] through completing 60 Professional Development Units (PDUs). PDUs can be earned through a number of ways, including in-person and online courses, attending webinars, or offering your services as a volunteer to particular organizations.

A PMP certification signifies your capability to speak the global language of project management and implies that you can perform as a project manager in almost any field or location, using any approach or methodology.

Plus, you're most likely to earn a higher income when you have a PMP certification; the PMI's Earning Power: Project Management Salary survey reveals that project managers with a PMP credential obtain a median salary of $111,000 in the United States, whereas project managers without a PMP certificate earn an average of $91,000[4].

2. PRojects IN Controlled Environments (Prince2)

The PRINCE2 certification can be described as process-based project management, as it provides a methodical approach to delivering successful

---

[1] Pmi.org - 2021 PMP Exam Content Outlines
[2] Pmi.org - PMP® Exam Updates
[3] Pmi.org - Maintain Your Certification
[4] Pmi.org - PMI Global Survey Reveals PMP®-Certified Project Managers Earn 20 Percent More In Salary than Uncertified Practitioners

projects through the use of clear templates, processes, and steps. PRINCE2 certification exam is administered by the APMG in the UK.

PRINCE2 is focused on both projects and processes: it is a broad, high-level, generic framework of project management principles, that specifies the roles and responsibilities of each member of the project management team. It also breaks down the master project plan into project plans, stage plans, and team plans, in order to eliminate ambiguity and make project execution easier.

PRINCE2 training is delivered by AXELOS' global network of Accredited Training Organizations (ATOs)[5]. PRINCE2 has two certification levels: PRINCE2 Foundation and PRINCE2 Practitioner. Both have different certification prerequisites. For instance, there are no specific pre-conditions for Foundation level certification. However, it is preferred to have a basic knowledge of managing projects but it is not mandatory. The prerequisites for the Prince2 Practitioner Level Certification exam involve passing one of the following: Prince2 Foundation, PMP, CAPM, or IPMA Level A/B/C/D.

The Prince2 Foundation exam duration is 1 hour, including 75 questions, with a required 50% pass percentage. The exam reference book is "Managing Successful Projects with PRINCE2". The Prince2 Practitioner exam is an open book exam (official PRINCE2 manual only) with a duration of 2.5 hours involving objective testing. The exam includes 68 questions with a 55% pass score.

Prince2 Practitioner certificate is valid for 3 years. After this term, you can either retake the exam to retain your credentials or renew it through an Axelos Membership. Additionally, to keep your certificate, you must earn and report 20 CPD (Continuing Professional Development) points per year for a 3-year period to maintain your certificate. Earning Prince2 CPD points fall into four categories: Professional experience, Training, Community Participation, and Self-Study.

3. Certified Scrum Master (CSM)

The CSM certification official provider is the Scrum Alliance[6]. This certification gives a comprehensive overview of the Scrum framework for agile project

---

[5] axelos.com
[6] Support.scrumalliance.org - How do I become a Certified ScrumMaster® (CSM®)?

management, including the fundamentals of the Scrum lifecycle, how to organize a Scrum team and set up the project, and how to manage releases and sprints, etc.

To undertake the CSM exam, you have to complete a Certified ScrumMaster course with a Certified Scrum Trainer (CST) first, either in person for two days (16 hours) or live online for 14 hours. Course attendance is mandatory to be able to obtain access to the online CSM exam and acquire the certification.

Candidates have one hour to complete the CSM test, which comprises 50 multiple-choice questions[7] based on the CSM Learning Objectives with a passing score of 74%. Students are offered two free attempts to pass the test.

The CSM credential is valid for 2 years. In order to maintain the certification, you must complete 20 Scrum Education Units (SEUs), and pay for a renewal fee. Attending relevant events, completing a Scrum Alliance course delivered by a Certified Scrum Trainer, volunteering to share your experience, and learning independently through watching presentations or reading books and blogs posts are all common ways to acquire SEUs.

4. Professional Scrum Master (PSM)

The Professional Scrum Master credential is provided by Scrum.org. The PSM comes in three levels: Level I involves the principles of Scrum mastery, Level II supports knowledge of real-world complex situations, and Level III addresses handling complicated teams and organizations.

It is not mandatory to take a course in order to be able to sit for the exam. You can take the PSM I assessment if you already have an advanced level of Scrum knowledge, as well as an understanding of the Scrum Guide and the way this approach is implemented. If this is not the case for you, there are numerous online courses available to help you prepare for the assessment and develop a deeper understanding of Scrum.

The PSM I is an online exam with a 1-hour duration to attempt a total of 80 questions. You must answer at least 68 questions correctly to pass. Once you

---

[7] Support.scrumalliance.org - What can I expect from the CSM® test? How many questions are there and what is the passing score?

get the PSM credential, there is no need for renewal as it has a lifetime validity[8].

5. Certified Associate in Project Management (CAPM)

The Certified Associate in Project Management certification is provided by the Project Management Institute (PMI)[9]. The CAPM designation confirms that you have a firm grasp on the key processes, terminology, and knowledge of project management. This degree can act as a stepping stone for beginners to get certified as a Project Management Professional (PMP).

The main difference between the PMP and CAPM certificates is that it's possible to get a CAPM without any project management experience, while PMP requires at least 4,500 hours of experience. You are eligible for the CAPM certificate if you hold a secondary degree (high school diploma, associate's degree, or the global equivalent) and you have completed 23 hours of project management education by the time you take the exam.

To retain the certification, CAPM holders must acquire 15 professional development units (PDUs) over the course of three years as well as paying a renewal fee.

Someone with little to no experience might decide to pursue a CAPM certification first, then work on gaining experience as a project manager to meet the PMP certification requirements. Someone with years of project management experience, on the other hand, usually chooses to go straight for the PMP.

Certification	N° Questions	Exam Duration	Pass Score	Exam fee	Maintenance	Renewal Fee
PMP	180	3h:50min	Not defined	$555	60 PDU / 3 years	$150
Prince2 Foundation	75	1h	50%	Varies with providers ($250 to $350)	60 CPD / 3 years	$210
CSM	50	1h	74%	Included in training ($300 to $3,000)	20 SEU / 2 years	$100
PSM	80	1h	85%	$150	Not required	$0
CAPM	150	3h	Not defined	$300	15 PDU / 3 years	$150

Most common project management certificates (August 2021)

---

[8] Scrum.org - Professional Scrum Master™ I
[9] Pmi.org - Certified Associate in Project Management (CAPM)®

***

Finally, we should emphasize that the certification you choose should depend on your job prospects and the region you are working in. For instance, if you need a certificate to prove that you've got some training, we recommend you go for CAPM. However, if you actually need a practical application of how to execute your job as a project manager, you should go for PRINCE2 or PMP certification programs.

Before making a choice, you should thoroughly review the prerequisites to determine which certificate is best for you. If you still can't decide which program will fit your career course, we recommend you do your research before choosing: thoroughly go through the displayed information about each certificate, and in case you know any certified or experienced PMs, you can ask them for advice regarding their own experiences and their recommendations.

Please note that there are many other project management certificates that are recently gaining momentum. We did not mention every certificate or credential out there, but this does not mean they are less significant. Taking into consideration the continuous emergence of new certificates nowadays, I can't stress enough how important it is to do your own research before investing any time or effort in a particular credential.

What are the most common project management interview questions?

Short Answer

Mainly, be prepared to get asked about your experience: the difficult situations and challenges you went through, types of projects you managed, the results you achieved, etc.

For instance, questions starting with "Tell me about a time you..." aim to assess your behavior. You should also expect competency questions directed to evaluate your technical and soft skills.

Explanation

Project management is recognized by senior executives and human resource managers as crucial for business success. Thus, skilled and qualified project managers are considered highly valuable resources among their organizations.

Yet, according to a survey conducted by the Project Management Institute (PMI), over $122 million is wasted in the U.S. for every $1 billion invested due to poor project performance. That's why recruiters can get exceptionally specific during job interviews and the recruitment process in general: Will the candidate fit into the culture of the organization? Will they get along with other team members and lead them effectively? Will they deliver the project goals on time?

Consequently, succeeding in a job interview can't be a coincidence: Yes, there are many unknowns, but being prepared for the interview by focusing on key areas and competencies as well as presenting convincing answers will eventually help you get selected.

In this section, we listed the most commonly asked project management interview questions along with pointers on how to properly answer them. The questions are categorized into two main focus areas: behavioral and competency assessments.

1. Behavioral questions

Questions such as: "Can you give me a specific example of how you did that?" and "What were the steps you followed to deliver that result?" are used to objectively measure past behaviors as a potential predictor of future results.

Sample Question1: *Suppose the customer is dissatisfied with the project outcomes. How do you deal with an unhappy customer?*
Answer: You should be able to explain how much you value your customers and that you can perfectly accept their authority. You can also add that in such a situation, you will try to make the necessary alterations that your customer is seeking while staying within the project scope. While explaining these steps, you should highlight the importance of using communication and negotiation skills for preserving a healthy relationship with your customer throughout the project.

Sample Question 2: *Name 3 skills or qualities that you think will make you a good fit for a PM position.*
Answer: You should be able to justify why you have chosen a particular skill. It's not sufficient to say that you are indeed a good communicator or leader. You need to cite at least one example where you employed these qualities in order to substantiate your choice. For instance, you can describe how you kept your team's motivation up in the midst of a distressed project or how you managed to resolve a conflict between your team members. Since communication is considered as the main aspect of project management, I recommend focusing on this skill by emphasizing how well you can develop healthy relationships among your team members as well as win stakeholders' support for example.

2. Competency questions

This area includes questions like "Explain a way in which you sought a creative solution to a recent problem you needed to solve." The purpose is to align your past behaviors with specific competencies that are required

Sample Question 1: *As a project manager, your team will often involve both on-site and remote members. Can you manage remote teams?*
Answer: The answer to this question mainly depends on your experience. If you have previously managed a remote team, then you can describe your own experience to be more accurate and convincing. Talk about the tools you used,

the processes you followed, and even the challenges you faced and how you were able to overcome them. If you don't have any experience managing a remote team, you should be transparent about it. However, you need to show that you're interested and comfortable managing a remote team (I assume you are). This topic is addressed thoroughly under the Communication & Leadership section.

Sample Question 2: *What is Agile? Do you have experience managing Agile projects?*

Answer: If the company you are applying to uses an Agile approach, then you should anticipate such a question. It's important to distinguish Agile as a philosophy from its different frameworks. Agile principles involve early and continuous delivery, adapting to changing requirements, and promoting collaboration and self-organizing teams. The most applied agile framework nowadays is Scrum which implies a set of defined practices and artifacts. The last section of this book is fully dedicated to Agile, which can provide you with the necessary information to properly answer this question. Even if you happen to have some experience with agile projects, it's important to keep abreast of new trends and updates by reading books or opting for online courses to fill in the gap between theoretical knowledge and practical implementation.

3. Other questions to expect

During an interview for a project manager position, you should expect a variety of other questions apart from the examples discussed above. Such questions aim to build a perception of your personality. Brain-teaser questions, for instance, are usually used to evaluate your mental calculation skills and creativity. Case questions aim to assess your problem-solving abilities and how you would react to potential scenarios.

Following is a list of the most common project manager interview questions:
- What did you like and dislike about your last project?
- Tell me about a time your customer wasn't satisfied. How did you address the situation?
- If your customer asks you to carry out a task beyond the project scope, how would you react?
- Is it a good thing to go above and beyond what is required from you?
- Tell me about a time you took initiative to improve a work process.
- What is your biggest accomplishment?

- Give me an example of a project that would have not succeeded without your presence.
- How do you evaluate a project's failure or success?
- What KPIs did you use in your previous projects? Were they efficient?
- What was the most difficult situation you ever went through during your experience? How did you handle it?
- Tell me about a time you missed a deadline. How did you react when you realized you were falling behind? What did that experience teach you?
- How do you manage stress? What about failure?
- What is the biggest team size that you managed or worked with?
- Tell me about a time when you had to mentor a team member.
- Tell me about a time you have disagreed with a senior staff member
- What would you do if one of your team members informs you that they prefer working solo instead of collaborating with the rest of the team?
- There has been a visible decline in the performance of a subordinate. How would you handle it?
- How do you maintain productivity during your workday?
- What is your leadership type? Or what is your preferred management style?
- How do your colleagues describe you?
- What motivates you?
- How does this job fit in with your career path?

4. Resources

The areas and questions mentioned above are not exhaustive. That's why we recommend a selection of books to help you prepare for your interviews:
- "Project Management Interview Questions Made Easy" by Andrew Makar
- "Cracking the PM Interview: How to Land a Product Manager Job in Technology" by Gayle Laakmann McDowell
- "60 Seconds and You're Hired!: Revised Edition" by Robin Ryan
- "Get That Job!: The Quick and Complete Guide to a Winning Interview" by Thea Kelley
- "How to Answer Interview Questions: 101 Tough Interview Questions" by Peggy McKee

Apart from books, there are plenty of soft skills programs and boot camps that focus on helping candidates pull off their job interviews. There are also numerous affordable, quality online courses dealing with this subject available on Udemy, for instance, or you can simply subscribe to certain Youtube channels such as "Work It Daily".

***

Preparation for a job interview doesn't happen overnight. From the time you decide to move to a new company or switch to a PM position, you should take a daily habit to read about project management and get familiar with the common interview questions. This will not just increase your knowledge sphere, but also increase your confidence during the time of the interview.

What's the difference between Project Manager, Product Manager, Business analyst, Project Lead, and Team Lead positions?

Short Answer

Usually, there is an overlap between all these positions, and job descriptions certainly differ from company to company. But, there are unalterable basics that make it easier to differentiate these roles, such as the fact that the product manager's main focus is on a specific product, and that the business analyst is mainly charged with defining project requirements.

In recent years, and in order to emphasize the leadership aspect of the position, "lead" was introduced to replace "manage" especially within IT startups working with the Agile approach. This is where the positions of Project Lead and Team Lead were brought in.

Explanation

Terms like Project Coordinator, Project Manager, Product Manager, etc are well heard in nearly all organizations. But, they often seem confusing for most people as they mainly struggle to figure out the distinctions and differences between these roles.

Though all of these positions relate and collaborate with each other, they have different responsibilities. In some organizations, all these roles exist. While in others one role may take up the responsibilities of other roles. For example, an organization can have a product manager with the responsibilities of a project manager as well. Or, a project manager can take the responsibility of a business analyst.

The same term or role may also have different requirements depending on the organization. For example, Google requires technical skills when they are looking for product managers. Yet, in Amazon, no prior development experience is required (Secrets of the Product Manager Interview by Lewis C. Lin).

Having a general understanding of these positions' responsibilities and limitations reduces the chances of confusion. Hence, it's imperative to understand the differences. So, let me break it down for you.

1. Project Manager

The Project manager is responsible for planning, managing, and steering the day-to-day activities of the project. They engage in managing and delivering projects end to end within the constraints of schedule, budget, resources, risk, quality, etc. They connect with the product manager to understand product features or requirements as they are the executors of the product strategies set by the product manager.

The product manager (in some cases, the customer or the sponsor will be filling this role) sets their expectations for the product while project managers translate these expectations to their team to act upon, to eventually ensure the product delivery within the stipulated agreements.

2. Product Manager

Product Managers are often addressed as the CEO of the products as they are fully involved with the product throughout its life cycle. In some organizations, they are called Account Managers.

A Product Manager (also called Product Owner) gathers feature requests, schedules releases, and coordinates sprints. They should be able to identify user needs, help a customer understand a business value, and work with cross-functional teams to manage product releases. Their effort is important for the company as they need to deliver products not just according to users, but the product that helps make the company vision reality.

A product manager is responsible for setting, prioritizing, and accepting the work generated by a team and ensuring the efficiency and integrity of all processes with respect to a specific product. They guarantee the delivery of products that the customer would appreciate and accept. They set the product strategy, translate the client requirements, and envision the products to ultimately bring them to life. They're involved in product costing and concerned with profit/ loss as they are responsible for product release and promotion.

3. Business Analyst

A business analyst takes care of assessing processes, determining project requirements, and providing executives and stakeholders with data-driven reports and recommendations. Business analysts assist organizations in improving their processes and systems by conducting research and analysis to provide solutions for business challenges along with helping organizations and their clients implement these systems.

Business analysts study a company's operations and make recommendations for enhancing its processes accordingly. This is often done with the aim of helping the organization make more money, addressing existing business issues, and/or achieving its objectives more efficiently. A business analyst's job is very closely related to the IT sector, and at some companies, business analysts are considered as technical workers operating within the IT department.

Nowadays, business analysts' solutions for their clients will usually involve the adoption of new or improved computer systems, and an analyst's role may extend to familiarizing the wider business with the benefits of this new technology as well as training colleagues on how it is used.

Typically a business analyst will communicate with the organization's senior executives to find out what they hope to achieve, develop ways to upgrade businesses based on past research data, convince internal and external stakeholders of the benefits a new technology or strategy can bring, supervise its implementation, and finally hold training sessions and workshops.

Key skills for business analysts include commercial awareness, communication and interpersonal skills, organizational and time management skills, problem-solving skills, analytical skills, leadership and management skills, and an interest/understanding of project management techniques and computing systems.

4. Project Lead

The project lead is responsible for leading the project work by engaging throughout the project life to lead the project team. Project leaders are more concerned with leading people during a project as a project's human resources are proven to be the toughest to manage.

Project leaders manage the team dynamics throughout the project to ensure the focus of the team on the project deliverables. Interested in project outcomes with their people, they show this interest to their team as well. They show this passion to walk the talk. They keep their team motivated and they ensure the team gets rewarded after successful project delivery.

The responsibilities of a project leader include setting the expectations for their team members, leading their team during work execution, acting as problem solvers in a project as they are responsible for conflict resolution, and reviewing and controlling the team performance to ensure the team is not straying from the goal.

5. Team Lead

A Team Lead is a mentor or supervisor who oversees a team, and who is usually of a particular specialization or area. A Team Leader's job purpose is to manage and lead a team of employees, communicate company objectives, safety practices, and deadlines to the team. They are also responsible for motivating team members and assessing their performance.

Team leaders encourage team members' development by identifying areas for new training or skill checks. They help with team member problems and oversee team member work for quality and guideline compliance as well. They take care of developing strategies to promote team member adherence to company regulations and performance goals.

Organizing team meetings to keep members up to date on best practices and expectations, as well as creating and sharing detailed and thorough reports concerning team performance, mission-related goals, and deadlines also falls under the team lead responsibilities.

People who get hired for this position usually have team leadership experience, employee training experience, product knowledge, industry experience, strong oral and written communication skills, interviewing skills, sales skills, motivational skills, and are result-oriented.

Apple, for instance, requires that a Team Lead has qualifications and experience in matters of team management, productivity and performance control, coaching, influencing, and leadership and creativity skills. Google requires the same qualifications as Apple for a Team lead position, with an emphasis on communication, innovation, and analytical skills.

6. Other positions

Other commonly found positions under the project management field include Implementation Manager, Stage Manager, Associate Project Manager, Project Communications Officer, etc.

***

Now that you understand the differences among these roles, it is evident that each role has its importance within an organization. However, it's not mandatory that all these roles be present under one company, as an individual may take more than one role.

What are a project manager's main duties?

Short Answer

It's so important to properly perceive your project success criteria. Your main duty as a project manager is to achieve the set goal, i.e., the business value. First, you have to fully grasp the project or the idea you're planning to execute, then you will be acquiring or given human and physical resources in order to duly carry out the project.

Along the way, you will be dealing with challenges such as quality, communication, risks, and budget constraints that need to be resolved. Many of these challenges could be avoided in the first place by implementing the appropriate process and documentation.

Explanation

Good project managers are usually people with an excellent entrepreneurial mindset, as it enables them to visualize a project beyond the basic skills required to lead it to the finish line. At the end of the day, the project's success or failure rests solely on the project manager's shoulders, and he or she is the one responsible for the end result. Project managers ensure that information and knowledge are flowing seamlessly. Thus, to keep the project on track, they need both technical know-how and first-hand knowledge of the tasks they assign to others.

"Project Managers play the lead role in planning, executing, monitoring, controlling, and closing projects. They're expected to deliver a project on time, within the budget, and brief, while keeping everyone in the know and happy."
— Cam Lee, Rock Agency

So basically, the project manager is the person in charge of conceptualizing, organizing, and executing projects within a company. They are expected to create comprehensive work plans, improve their team productivity, align projects to business goals, and constantly communicate project status.

Regardless of any additional responsibilities, the following four areas present the main duties of a project manager: Understanding the project, Acquiring and managing resources, Building and documenting processes, and Managing project constraints.

1. Understand the project

Whatever your role description entails, it's essential that you reach out to your sponsor, customer, and other stakeholders and gain agreement on the project objective, requirements, and evaluation and completion criteria.

You also have a primary responsibility of developing and using a realistic plan to track the work through to completion and acceptably achieve all requirements in a timely way. The proper execution of these tasks depends entirely on a thorough proper understanding of the project.

2. Acquire and manage resources

Planning is instrumental in meeting project deadlines, and many projects fail due to poor planning.

First and foremost, project managers are responsible for framing the project scope and determining needed resources. The word 'resources' in this context indicates the project team (people) along with the physical resources needed for the project such as equipment, servers, tools, infrastructure, etc. As a project manager, when acquiring resources for your project, you are putting to use two distinct sets of skills: how to recruit people and how to obtain physical resources.

Putting together a project team could be difficult when you are in need of the best talents, especially for mission-critical projects. Some negotiation, persuasion, and collaboration with other project managers, functional managers, and decision-makers in your organization will help you assemble the right team for your project. A project manager's ability to influence, network, and collaborate will get them a long way towards obtaining the required resources for their project.

Additionally, a project manager should set criteria for human resources selection and establish a resource management plan to figure out what kind of resources are needed, how many, and when they are needed. It's also important in your budget planning to include the cost of the resources recruitment, onboarding, and training, as well as their remunerations.

When it comes to physical resources, you should be familiar with qualified external vendors, consultants, and suppliers. The ability to negotiate prices will help you get physical resources on time and within the budget.

Skillful project managers know how to properly manage the acquired human and physical resources for the ultimate sake of the project's success. They should set realistic time estimates according to their teams' capacities. An efficient project manager should develop clear, straightforward strategies to stimulate their resources to attain their full potential.

Effective project managers also spend enough time with each team member to establish a strong bond. This is particularly difficult with distributed teams, but if you invest in frequent informal communications and periodic face-to-face interactions you can establish a connection even with distant contributors. Keep in mind that projects don't succeed because they are easy, projects succeed because people care about them. You must find some connection between what the project strives for and what each team member cares about to get all project contributors to buy into the project vision uncovering the "what's in it for me?" factor for everyone on the team.

3. Building and documenting processes

First, you should be aware of the processes mandated by your organization, and you should apply them unless you demonstrate to your management that the existing processes should be adjusted or skipped for your particular project.

Following your project needs, you can build more processes to improve communication, ensure quality, accelerate execution, etc. For instance, you can set up a process for collecting and sending regular project information and reports to key stakeholders.

I must emphasize that it's necessary but not sufficient to set up processes and get buy-in for them, you must also educate your team members and relevant stakeholders to ensure that everyone understands the processes they have committed to. You should establish appropriate metrics for process control and use them diligently to monitor work throughout your project.

Along with building processes, documentation should also be properly performed. Process documentation provides a detailed description of how a project process should be carried out. It should involve all types of documents that back up the understanding of its flow, such as policies, checklists, tutorials, forms, templates, flowcharts, etc.

For example, I developed the following flowchart, when I managed a team of developers, in order to demonstrate the process of managing tasks, aka issues, on Github's project kanban board. It did not just help my team grasp the whole process, but it has also fostered a smoother and easier process adoption by any newly hired members.

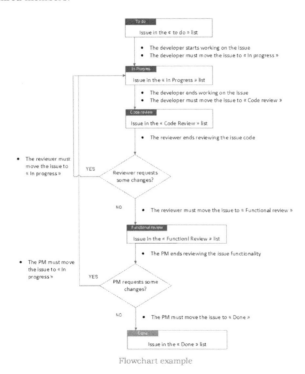

Flowchart example

4. Managing project constraints

The bigger the project is, the more likely there may be hindrances and issues that weren't part of the initial plan. A project constraint is anything that stops or puts a limit on your implementation strategies. A cost restriction in your project, for example, means that you are limited by the budget or resources available for implementation.

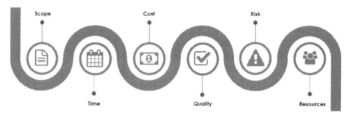

A project's competing factors

Since project constraints are often interrelated, changing one constraint will have an effect on the others. Such bumps are unavoidable, however, a good project manager will figure out how to meticulously and almost intuitively, detect and assess potential risks before launching the project.

"You have to go in expecting that things won't be as you had planned, and things won't be as easy as first expected. Goals, conditions, and circumstances will change." — Kalila Lakeworth.

The ideal way to handle project constraints is through transparency, implementation of project management best practices, efficient task management, and maintaining control over your project.

Transparency is usually regarded as a key factor for successfully managing project constraints. Transparency ensures that everyone involved in the process is aware of the project's priorities and objectives.

Implementing project management best practices and dynamic management strategies in your project is another way of dealing with constraints and completing the project successfully.
Creating a detailed work breakdown structure, measuring performance throughout the project life cycle, keeping the team members engaged, and

having an effective control strategy are some of the ways that can improve your performance despite the multiple constraints you might face.

To conclude, keep in mind that constraints are a regular and unavoidable occurrence in project management and that you are expected to deliver results nevertheless. In order to do so, you must be able to decide where and when you can make compromises on the scope, timeline, budget, or any other identified constraint. You can stay on top of things and deliver excellent outcomes by being ready and flexible enough to adapt and respond to changes and impediments.

***

To wrap up this question, let me emphasize that no matter how large or demanding projects are, you need someone who will reliably and consistently maintain efficiency and productivity. Project management is indispensable to successful businesses, and business owners need leaders with the right vision, the right skills, and the right know-how to face the biggest challenges and ensure projects are completed successfully and according to schedule.

Do you need to have technical knowledge of the project you will be managing?

Short Answer

Some technical knowledge is often favorable to acquire. A project manager should be at least conversant with the language of his technical team. If the project manager has zero technical knowledge then his team may give him unreasonably long estimates for tasks and inaccurate information taking advantage of his lack of technical mastery. On the other hand, when the project manager has in-depth technical skills, they may find it difficult to delegate and focus on their management duties.

Explanation

Should someone running an IT project have an IT background? Should a project manager leading a construction project have a construction or an engineering background for instance? Some people strongly think so while others do not agree. The answer is actually quite simple - it all depends on the project's size and complexity.

Technical work, whether it's hardware, software, construction, or infrastructure-related, is very different from project management work. It requires a technical background, training, and expertise in a particular field, in addition to the ability to use this experience to make technical decisions, often associated with the product of the project. Whereas, project management involves orchestrating the team's effort towards a definite direction in order to attain the project goal.

1. When you do need technical knowledge

When the project is small, the project manager may simultaneously take care of some technical work in order to create a balance. In such a case, the project is often neither big enough nor complex enough to completely separate technical tasks from project management duties.

Having technical knowledge may not be mandatory for a project manager, but it is favorable. A PM has to at least be able to speak the language of their team members as being technically clueless can lead to some issues such as inaccurate work deadlines.

While you are not expected to be an expert in all areas, you should be able to discuss the technology involved with your project as well as explaining to your customer or sponsor why a certain course of action was or will be taken and why it is beneficial. You may also have to make decisions based on reports from your technical experts. In addition, your ability to understand technical options will enable you to weigh them. In short, it definitely helps to have a technical background even though it's not 100% necessary.

2. When you don't need any technical knowledge

A complex or large project requires a full-time project manager. Additionally, the project teams are responsible for the technical work. Thus, they don't need someone undermining and second-guessing them.

In such cases, the project manager should be acting only as a General Manager. We all know what a General Manager's role is, and usually, they come from a management background not necessarily a technical background. But, if they do have a technical background, successful general managers make a conscious decision at some point in their careers to leave behind their technical background and embrace a new career as managers.

On a larger project, the project manager must remain focused on handling the project and all that it entails, rather than being distracted by the technical work that needs to be done. Also, the team should be large enough to involve technical experts.

This resulted in the emergence of a new breed of project managers, one that is particularly specialized and qualified in project management rather than the typically traditional project managers coming from a technical background. These people's entrance into the market is leveraging the profession as organizations are now looking for people with project management credentials and experience to lead projects.

***

Eventually, there will always be a demand for project managers with a technical background and for those with no technical experience: technical experts will still have a career path to become part or full-time project managers, and there will be a growing awareness and value placed upon those professional project managers whether they come from tertiary education, or they have made the decision at some point to be professional project managers.

Our tip for you is to not be afraid to move to another industry if you have solid project management experience, credentials, and a set of technical skills even if it may not seem to be an exact match to your aspired field; There are always common areas where you have the advantage of bringing a fresh perspective.

Should you take on a project you are not interested in?

Short Answer

Self-awareness is an important trait of a project manager. Realizing that you are not interested anymore in a specific project makes it hard to stay motivated and achieve the awaited results. That doesn't mean that you should believe in the project business case or get along with the sponsor in order to take on a new project. If you are mid-project when you feel like you're not really into what you're doing, then the right thing to do is to try and fulfill your engagement. If you can't do that, you can talk to your manager to resolve any issues and eventually hand over your responsibilities.

Explanation

Have you ever taken on a project that seemed like a good fit, but turned out to be a bad one? We are sometimes caught in some terrible fits where we need to dig our way out of the chaos. But how do you avoid getting into such a mess in the first place? and in case you're already into a project that you had no interest in or you lost interest in along the way, how should you act?

1. How to decide that the project is not for you

When you think about the project, are you excited to work on it? apathetic? already dreading it? When you're not interested in a project, at least mildly, your work on the project can suffer.

However, when you're excited about working on something, you are more likely to pay greater attention to details, go above and beyond to ensure that you're creating the best product possible for the client, producing something that both you and your client are proud to show off.

When you dread working on a project, either because you don't like the client, or the project itself is not what you are aspiring to be working on, then it's hard to stay motivated. The honest truth is that you're not going to love your job every day. Sometimes it doesn't matter how fun the project is, you'll have bad days. But, you should never work with someone who is such a bad fit that you have zero enthusiasm about the whole thing. It's not fair to you, and it's not fair to the client.

You should approach each potential project with the question, "Would I do this for free?" If the answer is a resounding "YES!" or "NO!" then you know where you stand. But more often the answer is somewhere in the middle. Take some time and really consider whether you want to do the project. Take money out of the equation. Is this something you would enjoy working on?

The third and most important question to ask is: Are you capable of the work involved? Sometimes, you might tend to underestimate the work involved, which will get you stuck and you might even need to hire someone to help you out. It happens, but you shouldn't go into a project that you know you're not capable of completing unless you have the full support from your managers.

Other questions that might help you determine how interested you are in the project are:
- Are you getting a fair remuneration for what you are doing?
- Do you communicate clearly with your project sponsor? Or do you usually get into an unproductive dispute with them?
- Are you both clear on the goal of the project?
- Is the timeline realistic?

Finally and most importantly, what does your gut tell you? As cliché as it might sound, most entrepreneurs and successful figures will tell you: you should always trust your gut. Sometimes you recognize that something is wrong, but you can't form the proper thought. Trust your instincts and avoid any project that just doesn't feel right.

2. How to deal with a project you are not interested in

This is the scenario where you took the project even though you were not interested in it, and now you're regretting it and looking for a way out. You're in the middle of the project and it's becoming a struggle to stay motivated and to be productive as a result of a lack of interest in the first place. So what should you do?

Here you have two options: either try to fulfill your engagements as professionally as possible and deliver the project as planned and take this as a lesson to never accept projects you don't have enough interest in or discuss the matter with your manager and/or client and explain your case as convincing as possible to eventually suggest handing over your responsibilities.

Handing over a project is not an easy task and it should not be taken as a simple one either. To ensure a smooth transition, you have to formulate a plan for handover including details to be transferred to the new project manager such as equipment and budget as well as indicating the progress reached so far and from which position they will be taking on the project. Next, you should set a meeting with the new project manager to discuss the plan and to gradually start the transition process. You might also want to meet project stakeholders along with the new project manager and introduce them to the project team.

***

It's an inevitable truth: enthusiasm can be inconsistent. This holds true for a number of things in life, but it is especially relevant when it comes to our enthusiasm towards projects. So, don't feel pressure or guilt when you lose interest mid-project, it happens. You should just analyze the situation to understand what caused your sudden change of heart to avoid getting into such stressful uncomfortable situations.

II. Business Challenges

Project managers encounter different issues related to their projects' unique business processes. Such issues usually involve operational challenges including the lack of an established process, delays, work overload, etc. Motivating your project team, framing and meeting expectations, as well as winning upper-management support all fall under this type of challenge.

Issues caused by inefficient management processes, for instance, will contribute to killing a project in the long run. Yet, the availability of resources, deadlines, training, and overall support are some of the most critical factors for the project's success.

Dealing with these common challenges is something every manager should be prepared for. With a smart strategy, you'll make sure that you properly handle these issues or even avoid them before they occur to get the most out of every single project you lead.

However, there's no simple formula you can directly apply for every business challenge you encounter that will yield immediate results, as every challenge is closely related to your project processes, team, budget, etc.

Under this part of the book, we will be examining in detail the different practical solutions, techniques, and tips to deal with the business challenges any new project manager will be mostly facing to help ensure the eventual success of the project.

Without further ado, let's get into it!

How to succeed in your first project with no previous management experience?

Short Answer

When you first manage a project, you may feel that the responsibility is overwhelming and that fear is crippling you when making decisions. To dissipate such feelings, you should rely on your strengths and showcase guidance and leadership in order to gain the confidence of your team, your manager, and your customer.

In order to make the optimal decisions, it's highly recommended to involve your team in the process. They will appreciate that, leading them to be more productive. One of the common traps for novice project managers is that they quickly jump in and try to do things themselves. My advice is, if possible, to keep this as an ultimate resolution and instead, try to delegate more efficiently.

Explanation

Your supervisor has called you in to ask you to lead your first project as a project manager. You might lack experience but it's not just luck that you've been assigned with the project. Most probably, it is a result of all the hard work you have been putting in as well as the skills and confidence that you are gaining over time.

While you are happy to take up the challenge and prove yourself, you are also scared of failure. Instead, you should think of it this way: If you can execute your first project successfully then it will establish your credibility as a good project manager. There are basic recommendations to follow to reach that success you're aiming for since project management has evolved nowadays into a process with defined stages and steps to guide those who are new to project management.

1. Gaining trust

Gaining the trust of other individuals involved in the project can form great support for a novice project manager. Yet, gaining your contributors' confidence can be a bit of a challenge if you are inexperienced with team leadership.

Even with the sponsors, managers, and significant stakeholders on your side, you still need to at least give the impression that you know what you're doing. Of course, it's always preferable to actually know exactly what you're doing, but at first, a minimum base of competence will suffice.

As a new project manager, your strongest asset for building and gaining your team's confidence and trust is generally your subject matter expertise. Think of it this way: you were assigned to lead the project because someone thought you were skilled enough to manage a project. Thus, work with what you already know well to always lead with your strengths. And, remember that "knowledge is power." Seek a few early victories with your team by simply defining your project's requirements, establishing processes, or carrying out the initial planning. People will begin to assume that you know what you're doing once the pump has been primed.

2. Involving your team in the decision-making process

Making decisions concerning your first project can prove to be a challenge. One way to make it easier for you is to involve your team members in the process, who in some cases, can exhibit a great deal of experience in project management matters. Just gather your team members and initiate a discussion.

It's always good to keep your team informed. If changes are being considered, inform your team about it as far ahead as possible to ensure that everyone is aware of the situation.

You can't win alone without involving your team. An experienced team can tell you if your plan is ill-advised and why, and if there are better alternatives. They can also help you get familiarized with the more technical aspects of the project and advise you on client interactions.

3. Delegating and monitoring work

One of the hardest things for a novice project manager to be aware of is that project leadership is a full-time job. Efficiently leading a project entails delegating project work to others, even if you are personally very good at it. You may be able to accomplish these tasks in a faster and better way than all of your team members, but you cannot hope to do everything on your own while also leading a project.

Delegating work to someone who might be less technically competent than you can be tough, even painful. But, you need to get over it. If you take care of substantial parts of the project work by yourself, you'll wind up with two full-time jobs: managing the project by day and dealing with project activities that should be delegated at night and during weekends. This will eventually lead to exhaustion, project failure, or both.

When you are making little progress at the beginning of the project, start monitoring what everyone is doing. That will make it easier to proactively identify potential issues before they turn into major concerns. For this reason, you should communicate regularly with your team to make sure that tasks are being executed as planned.

Communication can be carried out informally during team lunches and formally through emails and meetings to get the pulse of the team. Gather not only the progress status but also engage yourself by removing any roadblocks for the team when needed.

***

To successfully manage a project, you don't need to be an experienced project manager. You should, however, adhere to efficient project management practices to significantly increase the likelihood of your project success.

How many projects could you manage concurrently?

Short Answer

Realistically, most project managers are able to lead 1 to 5 projects at the same time. It entirely depends on the project size, its complexity, its process, business maturity, and finally the project manager's experience.

A full-time project manager often spends 35 to 40 hours per week working on a project, and if we subtract job-related overhead that isn't considered as project management or framework overhead, we'd be left with only 25 to 30 hours of work. Thus, concurrently managing multiple projects depends on the size and complexity of these projects as well as being aware of your limits.

Explanation

The number of projects a person can undertake at the same time is a relevant factor in strategic planning and in project portfolio management. Internationally, the de-facto standard states that a person should not manage more than two to three projects at the same time. But, several factors could affect this figure. Such factors include the project resources, complexity, workflow continuity, etc.

If you decide to manage more than one project simultaneously, how can you achieve that successfully? And when should you just stop and say: "That's too much" and maybe even decide to turn down new projects?

1. When to manage multiple projects

Managing more than one project properly requires either that the projects in question be small and simple, or that they do not require an uninterrupted effort. It is possible to manage more than one project if each is relatively small and the total number of contributors is approximately twelve or less.

Even when some of your team members are involved in more than one project, you should be able to keep things in balance as long as cross-project timing and resource contention conflicts are minimal. Plus, leading several teams of ten to twelve individuals working on separate projects requires an effective delegation of responsibility to leaders who can manage their allocated projects.

Such delegation is a key tactic in program management, which focuses on heading multiple related projects.

Regardless of how small the projects are, though, you should definitely keep the total number of simultaneous projects below five. You should also avoid taking shortcuts to take on more projects. Moreover, setting your priorities right by properly delegating tasks, for instance, will help you maximize your productivity and efficiency. We thoroughly discussed the proper way to delegate and prioritize your tasks under "How to effectively delegate?" in the Communication & Leadership section.

Managing more than one project can be more feasible when there are significant natural gaps in the work. Small projects that have a good deal of wait time in their schedules will allow you to easily manage more than one product at once.

Ultimately, the specific number of projects that can be managed concurrently fully depends on the complexity of the project, the proportion of work time to wait time, and most importantly your ability as a project manager to multi-task, delegate, and prioritize your work.

2. When to say "No" to new projects

Managing several projects simultaneously, where any or all of them might need attention at any time, often results in a loss of visibility and control and a probable failure of one or even all of them.

Project leaders typically spend about 10% of their time communicating with each full-time member of their project team(s), so communication in a project with a dozen contributors, for instance, will account for all of your available time. If you want to run more projects than your time allows, your organization will need to support you by allocating more resources to efficiently manage those projects.

Think of it this way: the more balls a project manager has in the air at one time, the more likely they will drop one or more. When managing several projects, you might fail to notice that one of them is heading for problems. Such mistakes can cause you some sleepless nights and harm your reputation as a project manager.

So, what can you do to avoid this kind of outcome?

Well, you should simply learn to say no and recognize when enough is enough. Don't take more than what you can actually handle. You will not only be stressed and overwhelmed, but you will also put your project at risk. Reporting the situation to your line manager will indicate good self-awareness, not incompetence as some may consider it.

***

When a project manager devotes all of their time and effort to a single project there's less risk of distractions or loss of focus which means a bigger chance of success. This isn't always the case though in today's business world where project managers must handle multiple projects at once. If that's what you're dealing with, just be careful not to overburden yourself and lose sight and control over your projects.

How much project management should there be on a project? Is there a typical ratio?

Short Answer

Again, it all depends on the industry, complexity, and size of the project. The ratio is also not flat since a project manager should spend much more time at the start of the project to set up all agreements and planning, and at the end of the project to verify the deliverables, close all agreements, and capture any learned lessons.

Some IT companies are using the 10% rule-of-thumb ratio which says that a project manager needs about 10% of the total hours dedicated by their team per week. For example, if your team is composed of 5 members, e.g., 3 developers, 1 quality engineer, and 1 designer, then the project manager may need an average of 20 hrs per week (5 members x 40hrs x 10%).

Explanation

The amount of time a PM should devote to managing their project depends on a number of factors as well as their personal preferences. Your superiors' involvement, your project status quo, and your personal judgment of how much time you can dedicate solely to your management tasks will all help you specifically determine and balance this ratio.

1. Project environment

One of the project manager's primary responsibilities is streamlining and implementing project management processes. A PM is required to develop project processes, improve existing ones, and document them by creating guidelines, policies, templates, etc. However, projects with an existing project management office (PMO) require less effort since all you have to do as a PM is just follow your organization's standardized instructions.

When your organization is too involved in your project management responsibilities execution, it results in more time dedicated to updating your superiors on what you're exactly doing, by filling out reports, communicating work performance assessments, participating in more meetings, and routinely reaching out to stakeholders. As it's part of your job to update your superiors on your activities, this close involvement will result in more time spent on managing your project.

Along with management involvement, having to acquire and develop a project team also affects your time allocation. Depending on whether or not you're the one directly responsible for the resources recruitment process, this task has a huge impact on the time you will be spending on managing the project. In case your organization has a dedicated department or person in charge of Human Resources, then you saved yourself a ton of time and effort.

But, even if you're not responsible for recruiting a team or you're already allocated the human resources that you need for the project, you'll still need to devote some of your time to train your team members in order to develop their skills when needed, as well as making sure to properly assign and designate each individual for their own well-being and the project ultimate success.

Along with human resources, a project also needs physical resources and it's your job as a project manager to handle procurements and sub-contractors. Your level of involvement in searching for the right providers, handling contracts, verifying the quality, and resolving related issues has a direct effect on your level of involvement in the project as a whole.

2. Determining your level of engagement

As obvious as it might sound, determining the exact number of working hours you are intending to dedicate to your project management is based on your own judgment and preferences. Taking into consideration the factors discussed above, you're the one to define your level of engagement in the project.

For instance, small projects with a short scope document, a few cost accounts, and a milestone schedule might only require a bare minimum engagement level. On the other hand, large projects including a detailed scope document, a Work Breakdown Structure (WBS), an elaborate and integrated project schedule, several cost accounts, support from a separate project control department, thorough progress reports, and so on, naturally require the project manager's continuous and full involvement and engagement.

***

Working as a project manager, you are assigned to a different number of tasks: meetings, planning, communication with customers, reporting to the management, etc. Ideally, you want to efficiently accomplish all of that in optimized duration. To attain this, you need to plan, manage and track your own work as well as your team's.

With poor planning and time management, it may be difficult to fit everything within the dedicated time you set initially. It might take some time to find the suitable ratio depending on your project environment and how well you're able to juggle your priorities, but eventually, and with some alterations along the way, you'll find the right balance that works for you and for your project.

How to handle a project with a limited budget or resources?

Short Answer

Most projects have similar limitations. In the worst-case scenario, your project almost consumes all of its budget while it's still under execution. A project manager should act before such a mess takes place. When some planning mistakes occur, the project manager should report them as soon as they are discovered. You can also consider some practices to lower costs earlier in the project like outsourcing work, educating the client to reduce expectations, and opting for a Minimum Viable Product (MVP).

Explanation

A project with a limited budget or resources can run into three major interrelated constraints: time, cost, and scope. The good news is that all of this can be tracked and corrected. Of course, the earlier you intervene the better.

No matter how tough the situation gets, as a project manager you have to ensure the successful realization of a project even with a tight budget. Luckily, it is practically possible to achieve your project deliverables without comprising many resources.
Here is how you can do it.

1. What you should do before the project starts

Before getting into the planning phase, you should clearly understand and identify your stakeholders' exact wants and needs. Give yourself the appropriate amount of time in order to gain an accurate comprehension of what everyone wants. It's a big mistake to rush into execution. First, try to identify whether you will be able to fulfill all of your key stakeholders' desires with your project resources or budget constraints.

Be transparent about the expectations and goals from the start. This way, you won't run into any last-minute costly surprises. At this point, you should put your negotiation skills into practice by educating your customers and bringing their expectations back down to earth.

Preparing an accurate budget and schedule estimates is also key to your project success. You should do that by using a detailed cost history based on previous projects. This way, your planning and estimations are based on previous precise data along with lessons learned, and we all know that lessons learned are a project manager's best friend.

Once your project plan is ready, you should identify which aspects of your project could be reassigned to the members of your staff rather than resorting to outsourcing as this might help you lower your project bill. You can also contact your vendors and contractors to find out if they can allow you any kind of flexibility with prices. If you have a good, long-established relationship with vendors, they might be willing to grant you more lenience.

Budget-wise, some projects have found the extra funding they need through crowdfunding, which not only addresses the cost issue but also acts as free marketing and community engagement. Of course, since crowdfunding is more convenient for small personal projects or prototype development, it is not really suited for all projects, therefore you should employ your best judgment here.

The key to smoothly executing your project despite the limited resources and budget is to plan accurately and smartly.

2. What you should do during the project

Getting into the project with limited dedicated resources and budget makes you want to be more careful throughout the execution phase.

First, you should resolve inefficiencies in your project workflow structure. This will not just alleviate both time and cost, but it will also help you avoid risks, errors, and reworks. Make sure that communication lines remain open, and that work progress tracking is up and running.

Second, work on building a cross-functional team. Being creative with resource allocation will help you avoid hiring new employees. You may not be able to acquire additional resources due to the limited budget, but that should not stop you from upscaling your existing team's potentials and skills through training, for instance, allowing you more flexibility when assigning them to different tasks and missions.

Remember that such challenging circumstances should not be a reason to settle for lower-quality outcomes. Not meeting requirements will lead your project to failure. Instead, if your customer's demands are out of reach due to the budget or resources limitations, you can renegotiate these requirements to try and convince them to lower the grade and adopt fewer features or functionalities for example.

***

Even though limited resources and budget can create a completely different way of managing and working through projects, you should take the learnings from such a situation. You will find out how to adapt your conventional ways of operating a project to adjust to unconventional circumstances to ultimately ensure success.

How to deal with work overload?

Short Answer

Work overload typically takes place when workers are being asked to complete an increasing amount of work, with fewer resources, and within less time. Such work conditions have left many project managers struggling to find ways to get it all done when it seems impossible.

The good news is that there are certain tips and techniques that you can apply to help you deal effectively with work overload. These tips can help you learn how to set limits, prioritize your workload, properly put to use all available resources, and talk to your superiors to create attainable goals.

Explanation

Work overload can have a huge effect on productivity, deliverability, and the overall work atmosphere. Yet, it can be avoided or solved by automating your work processes, ensuring that your communication is actually efficient, properly planning tasks through prioritizing and delegating, managing time to reach the best performance possible, and finally by learning to say "No" when you have reached your limits.

1. Automate processes

Not using technology in the workplace in the era when almost everything is automated would be a sin. As Louis Efron wrote in one of his articles for Forbes, "if leveraged correctly, technology has the ability to positively influence and support our humanity rather than push it away. It can help engage, recognize and protect those we care about and the people who work in organizations." He also suggests that technology should allow people to be effective, innovative but also stay connected at all levels, "it should facilitate the comfortable and expeditious flow of people, ideas and emotions."

Technology helps to address the negative elements in the workplace, replacing long, messy email threads, facilitating customer management, task and project management, and administrative activities.

Following are some of the most common tools to automate project processes:

- **Project management:** Primavera, MS Project, Jira, Asana, Monday, Trello, Tara.ai, etc.
- **Document sharing and collaboration:** Google drive, docs, sheets, Microsoft 365, dropbox, etc.
- **Communication:** Slack, Microsoft teams, Google chat, etc.
- **Video conferencing:** Zoom, Google meet, Webex, GoToMeeting, etc.
- **CRM:** Hubspot, Pipedrive, Zoho, Salesforce, close.io, etc.
- **ERP:** Odoo, MS Dynamics, QuickBooks, SAP, ERPnext, etc.
- **Code Management:** Github, Gitlab, Bitbucket, etc.

2. Use more efficient communication

One of the things you always have to be cognizant of is how you interact with your staff. You should always keep in mind that not all communication is effective communication. When giving directives, for instance, you should clearly state what your expectations are in terms of timeline and outcomes.

When working on a big project and the clock is ticking, clear concise communication could make the difference between meeting or missing your deadlines. When I worked on a rapidly growing web application project using the Agile approach, the product owner would frequently request new features stating that they should be treated as a high priority. In such cases, I follow-up by asking them how much of a priority is the new feature, "Is it required by the end of the day? by tomorrow? Or by the end of the week?"

One way to avoid work overload in your team is to understand what everyone is working on and to keep communication lines open. If your project follows the Agile approach, you will be syncing with your team through daily standups. Otherwise, try to make yourself available when people need to talk to you, giving your team every opportunity to raise issues when they need to. Even when everyone is busy, you need to dedicate time to keep in touch with your team as it may even help you avoid an unfortunate burnout situation.

Also, be sure to track work using some sort of system, even if it's just a simple spreadsheet. You need to have visibility of the work, so you can start to see problems before they spiral out of control. Traditional ways of recording work might have some limitations, but they do achieve their purpose. My dad for instance used notebooks to manage his construction projects and that worked pretty much well for him.

3. Prioritize, delegate, and manage your time

Instead of running around like a headless chicken, you should assess the situation to figure out whether your workload can be reduced in order to allow you to take some breathing space and focus on the most important tasks at hand.

The first step is to set aside some time, ideally outside of the workplace, and start working on a checklist of all the tasks that must be done and then classify them according to their urgency and importance. Sometimes, simply writing things down provides the required clarity.

Urgent-Important Matrix (Eisenhower Matrix)

Once that is done, start looking at which tasks can be delegated based on the available resources, as you may be experiencing a work overload as a result of your reluctance to delegate to those working under you. With a small workforce, companies must make sure to properly use and rely on every team member. Talk to your resources to find out how much available time each employee has. Once you realize which employees you can count on to deliver results, delegate tasks to them. But, remember that the ultimate responsibility still rests on you.

If you find that your own tasks are still overwhelming even after possible delegation, then you should consider asking your manager or immediate superior for help in prioritizing those tasks. They may give you some insights to get out of the situation, but if they don't, at least they'll be aware of it.

In the long run, developing proper time management skills enables you to become more effective and get more done throughout the day. Keep an activity log for a few weeks to see where you are spending your time, in what portion of the day you are more productive, and when you tend to be less effective. This will help you determine which areas require adjustment and improvement.

An example of a great time management skill is to set some time aside every day where you limit distractions, by shutting your office door, blocking your schedule from appointments, and turning off your phone. You'll be surprised at the amount of work you can complete when you eliminate distractions.

Another technique that I'm personally using to handle my workload and increase my productivity is developing an action plan using Google tasks. This helps me get a complete overview of what my workload involves, allowing me to determine if I'm going to be able to realize everything within the action plan.

4. Learn to say "NO"

This is one area that many project managers find challenging. You should learn to say "No" to activities that are not high up in your priority list or just eat up time without much benefit: It's necessary that you establish personal boundaries to only engage in activities that work for you.

Of course, there may be times when saying "No" can affect an entire process or project, so use this option with discretion. A huge step to dealing with work overload is to set specific limits on the amount of work you can handle. This may seem like common sense, but many find themselves accepting more and more work while increasing their workday to accommodate it.

The best way to determine what your specific limits are is to first understand your current workload. One way to specify this is to list all of your job responsibilities and how much time it takes to complete each task. This will provide you with an overview of where your time is mostly spent. Now you will be able to know what additional work you can accept, or provide concrete reasons as to why you cannot do any more work.

Many people struggle to say "No", and that's why their workload gets bigger and bigger. This can be even more difficult if it is your boss you have to say no to. Thus, it's crucial to be honest and let them know exactly what you are currently working on and why you just have no time to fulfill his request.

There's a common belief that opposing or disagreeing with your colleagues may ruin your work relationships or even your whole career. But, when you're being assertive, you're simply standing up for your rights.

One of the most critical communication skills at work is assertiveness. It entails finding the proper balance between passivity (not being assertive enough) and aggression (angry or hostile behavior). It also means having a strong sense of self-worth, as well as acknowledging that you deserve to get what you merit.

Eventually, there's nothing wrong with saying "No" when new tasks pile up on your to-do list. You only have to communicate with empathy and patience.

***

While pressure and stress cannot be completely eliminated, taking steps towards action areas that are within your control can help mitigate their impact on your professional life and even your physical and mental well-being. When work overload happens, it may be too late to quickly solve the problem. That's why it's better to prevent it.

Could a project manager also be a resource on the project?

Short Answer

There is a divergence in opinions concerning this matter; some are for the project manager being also a resource considering that it gives an insider look into the project, which allows them to spot any hidden risks, thus giving more accuracy to the project's status and schedule. Others are against such a possibility because of the conflict of interests that may occur, affecting the PM's objectivity and delegation efficiency.

Explanation

A project manager with limited to no technical knowledge obviously can't be a resource on the project. However, if they do have the required skills to work on some of the project tasks, they should be aware of the downsides of playing a double role in the project, being both a resource and a project manager.

In the first chapter, we discussed the duties of a project manager emphasizing that their main responsibility is to lead the project to achieve its fundamental goal. Since each project is unique, being a resource can be either a helping or an obstructive factor in attaining the project target.

Let me clear things up for you by identifying the major pros and cons of a project manager being also a resource.

1. Advantages of being a resource on the project

When a project manager has deep technical knowledge, it would be normal for them to get into the project as a resource too. An experienced Project manager who can separate technical and management tasks can help the work process when they get involved as a resource.

Being a resource on the team can give you additional insight into the status of the project which will eventually allow you to spot risks before they happen. You can also keep a closer eye on the schedule of the project.

Another major benefit of being both a project manager and a resource is having an unbiased viewpoint on the ideal way to address encountered issues and fulfill the project's objectives. You will get greater insights in terms of estimates and even be less dependent on resources to make decisions.

2. Disadvantages of being a resource on the project

Being a resource in the project you are managing may impact your ability to properly delegate as you might think you are better at executing some tasks than your team members.

Plus, let's not forget that managing a large project is a full-time job by itself. By being involved in task execution, you might risk falling into the trap of poor multitasking. As a result, the project's overall performance will undoubtedly suffer.

I recently managed two projects that lacked some resources in the design department. Since I have fundamental design knowledge, I jumped in and took care of those tasks in order to unblock the development team and deliver the required features on time. Even though I succeeded in delivering design features within deadlines, I had a difficult time keeping up with the other tasks that require my guidance and supervision.

***

Considering the way this question is labeled, my final answer would be that it's possible to have the project manager as part of the resources, but it's not mandatory for a project to be successful.

How to strike the right balance between project activities and support tasks?

Short answer

Managing the incoming stream of support tasks can take place by setting a ticketing system where the support queue is visible to everyone, by rotating the support group, or isolating a part of the team from interruptions while the other part takes care of support tasks.

Explanation

A bad balance between project activities and support tasks can affect team members' productivity and even cause frustration. There is no shortcut to getting rid of this issue. You have to primarily focus on protecting your team from unneeded interruptions. Then apply some tactics and techniques to effectively deal with incoming support requests.

1. Setting a ticketing system

The first and most obvious solution is setting a ticketing system. Ticketing systems (sometimes referred to as Help Desk), are one of the most important pieces of software used by top service providers and customer support operations. These systems allow teams to capture, handle, and track the status of customer issues in a highly organized and collaborative way.

Nothing feels worse than trying to solve loads of problems when you don't have a system to map out your action plan. A lack of organization can lead teams to be less productive, despise support tasks, and struggle with tasks prioritization. An online ticketing system keeps an organized list of prioritized tasks which helps support agents take care of support tasks more efficiently.

Because of the level of organization a ticketing system brings, requests won't require as much effort to answer. It'll also mean fewer hours needed to solve any problems. The efficiency will also mean reaching the balance you aim for between project activities and support tasks.

You can choose a ticketing management system that offers the ability to label tickets by expertise area as well as their level of importance. This will create an even more efficient problem-solving process by assigning issues to the right agents to handle.

I personally used Odoo Helpdesk in the past. It was an obvious choice at the time since the company I worked at was deploying Odoo as an ERP. My advice is to properly analyze your needs before opting for a solution that fits all your current and future requirements. Some of the most common ticketing systems include Freshdesk, Zendesk, Freshservice, Salesforce Essentials, LiveAgent, Zoho Desk, etc.

2. Staff rotation and teamwork

Setting a ticketing system can help, but it can't be a solution by itself. It can be a first step along with staff rotation practices and encouraging teamwork and collaboration among team members.

Creating a culture of collaboration and ownership among your team helps you resolve support tasks more effectively. When your team members tend to shirk or shuffle off responsibility, it is usually a concerning sign of lack of ownership.

You can adapt staff rotation to manage your support tasks where you can always isolate part of the team to focus on the project activities without being interrupted by support tasks. Staff rotation can be either based on a task-by-task approach or a time-related approach (weekly/monthly/quarterly support duties). Either way, make sure your team is aware that everyone is expected to help and take part in maintaining the balance required in the project.

If you're not comfortable with staff rotation or the support workload is fairly big, you can assign one to two people to solely deal with support tasks. They will be handling support levels 0 and 1 which involve receiving requests and performing basic help. The designated team can also deal with level 2 support tasks that require in-depth technical experience. But, in case they lack the needed technical mastery, they need to pass on the request to your project team to resolve.

***

Managing a team with implemented collaboration, teamwork, and commitment values will make support tasks easier to handle while your project is steadily running. And, it's not an exaggeration to ensure that such values will be key in facing almost any challenge throughout the project. However, you should remember that prioritizing quality in your project is what prevents getting a lot of customer requests and complaints in the first place.

How to win upper management support?

Short answer

Winning upper management support makes a huge difference for your project. So, here's how you can achieve that. First, try to be visible to the decision-makers in your organization. You should also be consistent while building your case, letting go easily will damage your credibility.

Finding a mentor, who can be an advocate for you and your project can help you reach high-level executives and win their support before and throughout your project execution. Work on your networking skills, as building a network of c-level influencing people can prove to be beneficial when you need support and guidance to get through difficult situations.

Explanation

One of the most common questions I get asked by new project managers is how to get the attention and support of their senior managers prior to project implementation. Management support for your moves and practices can make a real difference throughout the conduct of your project. Their support is vital for making key decisions such as allocating more budget to the project.

All successful projects have had support from senior-level management. However, sometimes management support is not easy to acquire. Try to connect to their goals and priorities, as this will help you find a common ground. Next, you can build your case by putting together case studies supporting your arguments. Being backed up by an advocate from management can also help you get the support you're seeking.

1. Be visible

Corporate executives don't usually know you in person. Even when they do have an idea about what your project values, they probably hold a neutral view about you, and this is where you should put in some effort to be visible to your organization's decision-makers.
Not being visible enough can get your project overlooked and neglected.

To stay on a forward course with your project, and to be effective in general, you need to have visibility and support beyond your team and your direct boss. You need people above and around you to see you as someone who matters.

When things get complicated, you need them to advocate for you or to come to your defense; otherwise, you and your project can get burned.

Apart from your boss, your clients, your employees, and your partners, your project gets influenced by other people who are not directly involved but still have a say in what happens to your project. So, you have two choices: either leave their perceptions of you to chance or proactively communicate with them and manage what they know you for. Leaving the perceptions of key executives to chance is one of the mistakes that can completely block your project from advancing.

Visibility is about getting your project out into the full sight of people who matter. You must let the right people know who you are and what your project is about, to eventually develop a favorable view towards you and what you're working on: take your show on the road and make sure you are not invisible. The trick is to create that opportunity to sell yourself to the decision-makers in your company. This doesn't always happen naturally, so it is up to you to create that opportunity.

Many people struggle with this idea of building visibility. But, no matter how you feel about it, you need to come to terms with the fact that you must do something to create positive visibility. In fact, you are building genuine value by getting yourself and your project on the radar screen. People with high positive visibility have high credibility, often getting all the benefits they aspired to in the first place: better projects, more resources, more support for who they get to hire, and better cooperation from other teams. As a result, they get better business results.

I suggest creating an actual communication plan to ensure that you're targeting influencers in your organization. You must have a clear view of who you want to have a positive impact on and create your strategy to be visible to each one of them. Reach out and specifically communicate what your project goals and desired outcomes are, and how they can help you achieve it all. Remember, talking in their language about things they already know and care about is what is relevant to them. Any planned communication will backfire on you unless it is relevant, competent, and trustworthy, and of course not boring.

Keep in mind when you request time or build communications to fit your communications into their context and be sensitive to the scope of what they worry about. If you try to get too much time for something that is not what they care about, you will lose credibility. As an example, I have found that with high-level executives you can build visibility just by requesting a short meeting. Request a five minutes meeting and briefly, and of course precisely, communicate your ideas, you may even be invited to stay longer as they will love you for being brief and right to the point. This will eventually build the visibility you need to actually win decision-makers full support.

2. Build your network and get mentors

Visibility, as important as it is, might not fully guarantee upper management support for your project. Knowing the right people who are willing to advocate for you will make things easier for you. If you are not good at networking, don't worry you are not alone. A lot of novice project managers struggle with networking skills. The good news is that you can actually do a good job at networking even when you are not naturally good at it.

Developing some key techniques to help or even force you to network will eventually back you up with a strong personal and professional network that will pay off in such situations where you need an advocate or a mentor on how to win your upper management support. After you try to network for a while, it will become easier and easier and it will start to happen more naturally.

That's the thing about networking. Everyone thinks they're not good at it, but in reality, you just need to do it to get better at it. Networking is not one of those things you can master by thinking about it. You just need to put yourself out there, do it, and learn as you go until you can build a strong network, even if you are uncomfortable or not naturally good at it.

Networking is about building a broad base of support for yourself, your team, and your project. Successful people are not isolated in their own world. They build the right networks of mentors, partners, and supporters. In fact, aside from your own efforts, mentors have a bigger impact on your success. Mentors help you connect at levels and places you would never connect with on your own. If, as a project manager, you are not sure what to do, talk to an experienced individual you trust.

You can either act big and pretend you don't need anybody's help, and risk failure, or get help, learn, grow, and succeed. Finding someone who has the experience to guide you through hard situations, and who believes in your project enough to advocate for you, will surely widen your margin of success. Asking for help actually builds your credibility: asking thoughtful questions and showing that you are learning creates transparency and builds trust.

Delivering a successful project at the beginning of your career without mentors is like climbing a mountain without protective gear. Sure, you can attempt it, but why would you? Without the help of mentors, you just can't work fast enough, at a high enough level of value, in a visible enough way, or more importantly, connect with the right influencers. Mentors provide a direct line to a level of people you might not otherwise be able to connect with. Sure, you need to be building your personal network directly, but mentors can expand your personal and professional network exponentially, not only in sheer numbers but also in usefulness.

When you ask mentors for a connection, you'll be amazed at what they come up with, and how willing they are to connect you with people who can provide referrals, recommendations, introductions, leads, sales, partnerships, all the things that make a project thrive. Don't get hung up on the term mentor. You don't need to negotiate a big agreement or formal process. You can just buy a coffee for someone you look up to and express how much it would mean to you if they can guide you through whatever you're struggling with.

3. Be unfailingly consistent

An inconsistent effort is a wasted effort, and an inconsistent personality is a big destroyer of trust. Each time you change your mind or your strategy, you destroy a little more trust.
The way to build trust in whatever you're working on is to select your priorities and stick to them. Sticking to a strategy or an idea gets stuff done, and seeing the progress you're making is a huge trust builder.

For instance, the more you communicate, the more comfortable people will be with what you are suggesting. Consistent communication builds trust. Lack of communication or inconsistent communication, however, destroys trust. You should communicate more than you think is necessary, while making sure your messages are clear, straightforward, and brief. Be relevant, concise, and useful. Then repeat.

The hardest part about building trust is that you need to be unfailingly consistent. As soon as you let up, change your mind, disappear for a while, don't pounce on a consequence, let something slide, fail to give credit, or back off on communicating, you are degrading trust. When you let people know what to expect from you because you behave consistently, you build up credibility and trust with them.

***

Project managers have a difficult job. By the nature of their role, they assume responsibility for pursuing and succeeding with new initiatives. One of the most important factors in promoting a project's success is the constant presence and the effective support and engagement of the upper management.

In most organizations, it's necessary to gain the support of decision-makers to move forward with any significant project as they are the gatekeepers for making changes. While not always the easiest task to accomplish, following the above steps will help you get this level of management on your side. Initially, you should keep them informed and show them the importance of getting your project off the ground.

Since their role is one of the important pieces of the puzzle for project initiatives to succeed, successful project managers understand the importance of this role and constantly work to gain the needed support at the right level and intensity.

What to do when your project sponsor leaves?

Short Answer

It is common for projects to experience the sponsor's exit. This should be avoided in the first place by keeping the sponsor as actively involved as possible. To accomplish this, project managers should meet with the sponsor regularly, keep them informed of project progress, and frequently ask for direction and advice.

Unfortunately, even an engaged sponsor sometimes leaves mid-project. If the project is still important to the client though, you should be able to continue the work, if not, you should probably cancel the project due to lack of sponsorship.

Explanation

Of all the things that could go wrong in a project, the one the project manager has the least control over is the sponsorship. In today's rapidly changing business environment, it is not unusual for companies to experience turnover of key project resources such as the project sponsor. Sometimes as the project progresses, sponsors move on, lose interest, or simply disengage from projects that they initiate.

Strong sponsorship is required for a project to be executed successfully. So, if you do lose your sponsor, you should urgently work on solving this issue. There are numerous solutions to keep the project on track, and if you've got what it takes, you may even be able to transform this crisis into an opportunity.

1. Avoiding sponsor exit

Typically, a project would not get funded or started without a sponsor. However, in some projects, the sponsor tends to sink into the background and does not remain actively engaged in the project. When this happens, the client simply starts to lose interest.

Good project managers should make sure this never happens. The sponsor should be kept as actively involved as possible. To accomplish this, project managers should meet with the sponsor regularly, keep them informed about project progress, and frequently ask for their direction and advice. You should always make sure your project has full support and attention from the sponsor.

When you start noticing signs of disengagement or lack of interest, you should discuss it with the sponsor. A strongly built relationship between the project sponsor and the project manager might even lead the sponsor to give you an early notification in case he's leaving the project so you won't be surprised and you'll have time to analyze the situation and act accordingly.

2. Inspecting client interest

Sometimes, no matter how hard you work on keeping your sponsor engaged and interested, they leave anyway due to various reasons. Such an exit has a big impact on the client interest and willingness in the project continuity.

The worst thing would be to continue the project without business involvement and then have to redo much of the work later on, or even cancel the whole project for lack of sponsorship. Transitioning from one sponsor to another can lead to a lack of focus from the client organization. When a client is not as engaged as they should be, it manifests itself in the form of unanswered phone calls, unreturned messages, missed meetings, or missed deadlines.
In this case, the loss of focus from the client is directly related to the loss of the project sponsor.

Avoid keeping things going based on their own momentum: Make sure to revalidate business commitment from your client, and make sure you are still on the right track, then you can refocus the team for the next phase. If the project is still important to the client despite the sponsor exit, you should be able to get a new sponsor involved, reenergize the client group, and continue the work.

If the client is no longer showing interest, you might need to put the project on hold. It would be a potentially painful step, but not as painful as it might be for your company to complete an irrelevant project. Once a client understands that a project will be put on hold, they will have to make a decision on its relevant importance: if it is important enough, it will receive the proper level of focus, if not, the project will probably not be continued.

3. Stopping the project

It's not easy to stop a project, especially since the resources allocated to the project could become idle or could potentially be reassigned. However, you cannot continue without an identified sponsor or client commitment. Without an active sponsor, you might be able to keep the project going in the short term but almost always this will result in a less than the optimal solution from a business perspective.

This is where you should consider euthanasia: when the sponsor leaves, the project usually begins falling apart. In that case, you're better off killing it than letting it drag you down.

***

When your project sponsor leaves, try not to panic to avoid making impulsive, often incorrect decisions. The best preventive step you can opt for is being alert to signs of disengagement to quickly act when you see your sponsor losing interest.

Try to step in early to talk to your sponsor so you can avoid a costly project failure – both in business terms and in terms of your personal career. You may want to dig in and find out why their engagement and interest are fading and switch up what you are doing to bring them back on board.

III. Communication & Leadership

Active communication and effective leadership has never failed anyone.

Arguably, the lack of and/or incorrect communication is the most common underlying cause of any company's issues. Effective communication isn't only about managing workplace conflicts; it's also an essential factor in building solid relationships with your clients, boosting your team's effectiveness and engagement, and ensuring profitability.

In addition to communication struggles, project managers are often faced with particular leadership challenges too. They're charged with executing projects successfully while also managing budgets, obtaining stakeholders' support, negotiating contracts and vendor agreements, supporting strategic initiatives, and developing their employees' skills and expertise.

In order to successfully avoid the usual pitfalls, we are going through these communication issues and how to resolve them, empowering new project managers through effectively developing and running projects and acquiring a communication and leadership skills set in the long term.

How to motivate your team?

Short Answer

So, you've hired some talented resources, and now you need to make sure they stick around. You can achieve that by sharing your vision, setting clear goals, providing feedback, showing appreciation, creating a rewards system, laying out opportunities for self-development and growth, and keeping open communication to provide support when needed. Leveraging autonomy by avoiding micromanaging your team can also help a lot.

Explanation

Keeping your team motivated throughout the whole project is among your duties as a project manager. While money and benefits are certainly important, studies show that they don't top the list of motivation factors. Instead, some of the more important motivators involved feeling recognized, being encouraged, and having growth opportunities.

1. Sharing a common vision

Having a meaningful and worthwhile goal can be a huge motivation for your team. While defining a common vision is relatively straightforward, persuading others to follow it is the real challenge.

You should frequently communicate the project or company vision to eventually convince your team that they are part of it. Of course, you cannot force them to conform. However, adhering to the defined vision will make you a strong source of influence.

2. Setting clear goals

You can only motivate and inspire your team if they know what they are working towards. Make sure your team is aware of what the ultimate goals for the project are and their own goals within it. Don't say "Our goal is to rank first on Product Hunt", instead "Since our goal is to rank first on Product Hunt, you should come up with a stunning product design".

Having insight into how the project is going makes your team more invested. So, make a point to share this data with them on a regular basis. This will make your team members realize how crucial they are as part of the project, as well as helping them identify and address any areas of improvement.

3. Delegation and autonomy

As an important and broad subject, delegation will be addressed in a subsequent section to thoroughly highlight its importance and how it should be done effectively.

Supporting team members when dealing with work issues will eventually lead to autonomy. Openness and direct involvement of your team members in the decision-making process is another critical step in motivating them. As their confidence, commitment, and competence increase, you should start delegating more work to your team and allow them to make decisions and solve the issues they're facing.

4. Acknowledgment and rewarding

Sometimes all people want is some recognition for a well-done job. Team members whose achievements are recognized express a higher level of satisfaction with their work. But, if they feel that their long working hours and personal sacrifices were in vain, they are unlikely to go above and beyond for the organization or the project. It's important that you express your appreciation and gratitude to your hard-working team members, whether mentioning their contributions in a meeting, recognizing their efforts in a staff email, or simply thanking them in person.

Years ago, I was working as a project manager in the telecommunication field. Once, while I was leaving the office at 5:30 pm, my colleague Wafa was still working overtime on some design tasks for another project. The next day, as we were chatting, she told me that she stayed until 7:30 pm at the office to complete the pending work. I was really impressed by her dedication, "It's exceptional that you stayed that late even though you didn't have to. Seems like you're doing a great job". She was instantly delighted by my comment, replying "Alhamdulillah (thank God) for having my effort acknowledged by someone. I was really disappointed that my manager didn't say a word about it."

In addition to compliments, you might want to consider starting an incentive program. If people know they'll be rewarded for a properly done job, they'll be more likely to perform well and stick along to see things through. Depending on your project length, you may want to opt for a quarterly, milestone, or project success bonus.

Keep in mind that it does not always have to involve a monetary reward to motivate your team; simple things like an appreciation "Thank you!" email will be sometimes sufficient.

5. Communication and growth

Instead of trying to guess what matters most to your team, sit down with them to find out what they truly value. Spend a few minutes every day talking with your team members, discussing everything from concerns to ideas. You will be amazed by how much insight you will have on what's going on with your project and within your team.

This might seem obvious, but poor management is one of the main causes of employees' dissatisfaction. It's your duty to coach, mentor, and assist them through solving their problems instead of referring issues to you to handle.

Your team members will be more efficient and valuable to your project when they're provided with opportunities to develop new skills. Offer your team the training they need to boost their careers and refine and upgrade their knowledge about the latest technologies and industry updates, and you'll be amazed by the impact on their self-esteem and performance.

***

Motivation is a crucial component of a healthy workplace, thus you should constantly strive to make your team members feel appreciated and inspired. As you come to know the people in your organization better, you'll be able to fine-tune your motivation strategy. Subsequently, they will reward you back with increased devotion and a positive perspective for the future of the company.

How to convince your team to adapt the project management processes?

Short Answer

Selling people on good project practices might be hard but it is not impossible. You can deconstruct your team's change resistance by successfully communicating and demonstrating benefits, emphasizing the importance of conforming to standards when adapting the processes, and even customizing these processes based on your team's feedback and suggested alternatives.

Explanation

You've done the research, compared and demoed a shortlist of project management processes, and now it's time for implementation. Easy, right? Not really. Implementing changes, particularly with large teams, is a monumental mission that must be approached methodically and thoughtfully. Resistance to change happens even in forward-thinking organizations. Getting your team on board with adapting project management processes is no different than asking them to adapt to other changes, and takes time and effort.

Fortunately, there are numerous strategies you can utilize to turn skeptics into keen supporters. We've got a few steps to help you implement your PM process, but in order to successfully do so, you have to understand where your team members' resistance is coming from.

1. Demonstrating benefits

To get your team members on board with any type of change, you need to successfully communicate what's in it for them. For instance, perhaps your current process wastes their time and effort. So, explain that the new project management process will recover this lost time and prevent tasks from slipping between gaps. Demonstrate how it will help your team work smarter, not harder.

Project situations vary, but when contributors push back on the use of project management processes, it's usually based primarily on the fact that the processes require more work. The assumption that employing good project management practices will lead to more work is generally untrue. Projects, where there has been little planning and control, are almost always full of regrets. Try to surface the issues that bother your staff and show them that the overall work using appropriate processes will be less, not more.

In one of my past work experiences, we have set up a process where two developers were assigned to review the code before it gets merged with the product code. This quality measure improved the product code quite a lot resulting in fewer technical problems and fewer meetings throughout the project.

2. Conforming to standards

Some types of projects have governmental regulations that mandate certain processes, and others must adapt them either for industry compliance reasons or to remain competitive. If any of this is true for your project, point out to your team members that in addition to project management practices being a good idea, there will also be significant consequences if you fail to adopt them.

Even if there are no external standards or regulations available to help you enlist cooperation, there may be organizational requirements you can cite. Project management or program management offices often set up mandatory processes, and they may also install "process police" to monitor what is going on and help to ensure appropriate adoption.

Although practices adopted to comply with prevailing rules are easily implemented, they may or may not always be entirely appropriate. Exploit any help this provides, but also monitor your results and consider alternatives if you find that obligatory processes are ineffective.

Over time, use your post-project lessons learned, discussions with your sponsor and management, and work with your peers to adjust your mandated processes so that they will be a good fit for your project.

3. Customizing the process

Instead of introducing all aspects of the project management process at once, you should limit it to a few simple functions at a time. This will get your staff used to the overall "look and feel" of the process and create an increased level of confidence before they move on to any serious training. You can also gamify the onboarding process so team members receive small rewards for their progress.

Make sure the small tasks you assign are useful and try to continuously highlight and demonstrate the process' benefits. It is always better to have people adopt practices that they are convinced of rather than demanding that they do so they are obliged.

Involve your team members in fine-tuning how you plan to proceed, and listen to their feedback. If there are major objections to the processes you are recommending, ask those who are complaining if they have other alternatives. If they come up with options that appear better, you should consider them. If there are no better options voiced, ask if opposing members would at least try things your way for a while to see how it goes.

***

Eventually, asking questions to guide the discussion with your team can be effective to convince people that processes are in fact desirable. Help people see for themselves how good project management practices can address and resolve their problems. Success stories can also be compelling. So, try to identify similar projects that have succeeded using practices you would like to adopt and build the case for emulating what they have done.

How to manage remote team members with different time zones?

Short Answer

Nowadays, your project team is likely to be scattered far and wide. Being spread across the world makes collaboration and communication more challenging. Establishing the trust and camaraderie that a high-performing team depends upon is most difficult when people are not located together. Luckily, there are things you can do to help through team building, maintaining good relationships, and avoiding favoritism.

Explanation

Nowadays projects can't always co-locate, so you need to do what you can to properly manage remote teams. This can be done by adapting the adequate work methodology and approach, providing your team with enough flexibility scheduling and planning-wise, trying to encourage teamwork, and maintain relationships despite working remotely.

Being clear on your expectations and setting clear goals for your remote teams can ensure smooth functioning. Additionally, technology offers multiple tools for dealing with this challenge by ensuring efficient communication despite the different time zones.

1. Flexible scheduling and regular meetings

Flexibility is mainly what attracts many employees to remote work. Studies show that flexible schedules make employees both happier and more productive. According to a US nationwide survey, 65% of remote workers feel that telecommuting increases their productivity. 86% indicated that working alone allows them to achieve their optimal productivity. Also, these flexible schedules usually create a strong home/life balance as compared to onsite work.

Team members should be given the flexibility to set their own work hours and the freedom to design their own schedules, which will enable them to be most effective. However, strong communication is vital with remote team members who may sometimes feel invisible and isolated when their work hours don't overlap with their colleagues' schedules.

Regular meetings can be a suitable opportunity to connect with your team members and trigger purposeful engagement among them. When I worked for Foretheta last year, a remote-first company, we had a bi-weekly meeting called "Coffee Time" to chit-chat about everything except work. We had a lot of fun during these meetings where we were able to get to know each other more, share memorable discussions, and create more intimate strong team bonds. Nowadays, a lot of remote companies go for similar concepts. For instance, GitLab sets up a "Coffee Chat" meeting where collaborators are paired with people from different projects or regions to broaden their perspectives.

2. Establishing and maintaining relationships

Nothing works better for team building than meeting face-to-face, so if at all possible find a way to bring people physically together, at least briefly near the beginning of each project. The most common justification used to do this is a project kick-off or launch meeting.

If you are unable to gather everyone, at a minimum bring subsets of the people who will work on your project together, and travel to join them. If all else fails, video conferencing would be the best feasible alternative.

Strive to establish linkages between your team members, building on common interests such as educational backgrounds, common acquaintances, and anything that helps the folks you are working with see each other as colleagues and friends.

Share pictures of each other, ideally taken in recreational or other informal settings that will show that this is not just about the job at hand. In this digital age exchanging photographs is easy, and posting them on communication platforms such as Slack or Microsoft Teams will reinforce that everyone is human and that you are all in this together.

In hybrid companies, it is especially important to motivate geographically distant contributors and to connect them to your local team. Work to discover something about the project that matters to your remote team members, such as the type of work they prefer, aspects of the project that are personally important to them, or anything else that can increase their motivation and buy-in. Above all, reinforce things that you all have in common, and strive to break down barriers and minimize any differences.

3. Being clear on expectations and targets

Because you won't be as available to remote team members, it is important that you are clear about what you expect. Setting objectives and summarizing actions for each day, week or month will help you keep everyone in the loop while ensuring that all employees are aware of what is expected of them in terms of delivery, regardless of whether their working hours overlap with yours.

I used to manage software projects using the Agile approach, Scrum more precisely. Apart from having daily standups to address and remove any impediments, I continually reminded my team that they can send me their inquiries at any time and I will respond as soon as I'm available. If a deadline is communicated, I always include the timezone so members from different regions don't get confused. For example: instead of saying "the newsletter is due tomorrow morning", I would say "the newsletter is due tomorrow morning PST". For more urgent stuff, I sometimes define the hour; "the newsletter is due tomorrow at 10 AM Pacific Time".

4. Adapting helping technologies and tools

Asynchronous communication is really important with remote teams. It ensures that everybody knows who is working on what, and when. This means that projects flow smoothly, things happen on time, and blockers aren't left unaddressed. Plus, it cuts down on distractions.

Trello, for instance, allows you to track your project as it enables your team to update the board cards when they make progress on a certain task. Its Kanban board feature represents an information radiator for all the team. The same feature is also available in Github under the project menu, and it could be configured as follows:

- **Backlog:** for tasks in draft mode. It can include any wanna-be feature or any discovered non-critical bug.
- **To do:** for approved-for-execution tasks.
- **In progress:** as soon as the developer starts working on a task, it should be moved to this column.
- **Code review:** when the developer finishes a task, it should be placed in this column to be reviewed by other developers.
- **Functional review:** once developers approve the code, the task should be moved to this column for another step of verification.
- **Done:** once everything is checked, verified, and approved, the task is moved to the "Done" column.

Real-time chat tools like Slack or Microsoft Teams are also a must. They can be used for brainstorming, asking each other questions, passing files back and forth, comparing notes on new releases, and much more.

Other really helpful tools you can use along with your remote team include World Time Buddy for easy meetings planning. World Time Buddy can help you find overlapping time zones when you're trying to schedule things in advance. Below is a World Time Buddy configuration for a remote team located in London, New York, and Islamabad:

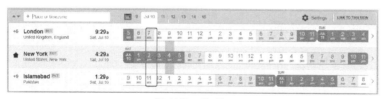

World Time Buddy

When your project team is located in different countries, it means that they have different holidays. This is where Google Calendar comes in handy. Having a shared Google Calendar where team members mark their vacations and local holidays, could help a lot planning-wise. Google Calendar comes with a great feature which consists of automatically adding national holidays to your calendar in just a few clicks; on your left, next to "Other calendars," you can click on "Add other calendars", then "Browse calendars of interest", and just check the country you're interested in or where your team is located.

***

Keep in mind that team members without a physical presence can end up having a smaller voice by default and it is far easier for people in the room to jump into the conversation than when you are on the end of the phone. Always ensure that everyone is included in the conversation to prevent individuals from feeling undervalued.

How to run effective meetings?

Short Answer

Frequent unnecessary meetings can waste everyone's time, reduce effectiveness, and simply be boring. Consider using alternatives such as emails and calls if the outcome of the meeting can be delivered through those mediums. Setting up an agenda may provide more details on the meeting and whether it's necessary or not. Plus, adapting daily updates as a habit can prevent unnecessary meetings in the first place.

Explanation

It's important to give your team the mental and emotional space that they need to be productive. Not all meetings scheduled actually need to be meetings, taking into consideration that everyone's time is precious. But, how can you reduce unnecessary meetings? If you're hosting or participating in too many meetings, here are four strategies you should implement to reduce unnecessary meetings and free up the amount of time you spend in conference rooms.

1. Setting a clear agenda

If you've already had a meeting to plan and structure the work, spend some solo time thinking strategically: evaluate the scope of work and the current progress toward milestones, and you should be able to start figuring out your action items and other progress that must happen. Then, ask yourself if the outcome you want from the meeting could be achieved through an email or Slack? If the answer is yes, you should consider trying to use those mediums instead.

Once you decide to organize a meeting, you should set clear goals beforehand. Having the goal in mind, attendees can easily focus on the goal and get things really done. However, we all know that during meetings, new aspects arise and lead the discussion to go astray. In this case, you should cut the discussion and put the item on a list of side issues that should be taken care of in the next meeting. For instance, you can redirect the discussion by saying "Guys, let's focus on today's topic and tackle this issue on another occasion". The key takeaway here is that a well-prepared meeting could help you avoid wasting your time and effort on several impromptu and unfocused meetings.

For meeting invitations that don't have a written agenda, you should ask the meeting organizer to add one. By doing this, the agenda may provide more details on the meeting and whether it's necessary for you and for your team to interrupt your work in order to attend the meeting.

Google Calendar has made it ridiculously simple to send an invite to your colleague's calendar. Google even has a feature that proposes a time when you and your coworkers are all free to set up a meeting. But, just because it's very easy to organize a meeting doesn't mean you should hold one whenever you feel like it. Therefore, you should implement the following policy: If you schedule a meeting, you must create an agenda first. Otherwise, the meeting is a no-go.

When you require a meeting agenda, you force the meeting planner to stop and thoughtfully consider the purpose of the meeting, who should attend it, and whether it's even necessary at all. Sure, it adds a bit of work to the host's plate. But, that's the point. If the meeting organizer can't or doesn't want to create an agenda, it's likely the meeting won't be valuable. Not only does this leave you with fewer meetings, but also, when you do have a meeting, everyone will be better aligned.

An agenda enables you to decrease the lost time at the beginning of each meeting as everyone enters the room with an overall understanding of what subjects will be covered, thus they know how to prepare for the discussion and contribute to the decision-making process. That way you can address any issues and efficiently make decisions as planned. The meeting will also be more likely to stay on track since the agenda will serve as a resource for the team to refer to even after the meeting is over. So, this way, everyone wins.

2. Time framing

Without having a clear time frame to work on a topic (aka time-boxing), people tend to babble and tell stories. But, since everyone's time is precious, you should set time boxes for each topic you plan to discuss and track them by a prominent clock.

Before organizing a meeting, you should identify the meeting's time frame. What kind of meeting time is needed for the meeting's purpose? Different time frames fit different purposes: from the five-minute daily check-in to the two-day retreat. So, make sure to match the amount of time to the needs and the frequency of the group's gathering. Moreover, allot time frames by topic. Considering the total time available, assign realistic time slots for each item.

Make personal notes on each of the agenda items and consider the items' priority to allocate time accordingly. Also, when starting the meeting, you should state its purpose and desired outcomes and restate the time frame: if attendees know there is a strict end-time, they will be more likely to stay on track.

During the meeting, make sure to stick to your allocated time frame for each item as a good portion of running a successful meeting is time management. If the group hasn't reached a decision within the provided time, suggest the next steps or refer the item to the upcoming meeting.

3. Setting a frame for regular updates

With remote work, clear and concise communication becomes essential. For instance, think of designating a time during the day for your team to have a short recurring daily meeting: a lot of what could be mentioned in a scheduled meeting could be discussed in a short daily meeting first. If the topic needs more time to be discussed, you should then consider scheduling a follow-up meeting if necessary.

You can opt for two kinds of meetings for your regular updates:
1. **A daily huddle** is a 5-10-minute daily meeting to sync with the whole team where all of you share the tasks ahead of you for the day and make general announcements often about office events, updates, etc.
2. **A weekly all-hands** is an hour-long all-hands meeting. The format of this meeting includes updates from every department (often including demos), good news updates (both personal and professional), financial updates, and a Q&A session to clarify any issues and inquiries.

These two meetings may seem like a lot of commitment, but it's worth it as they will save you hours of additional meetings that would need to occur due to a lack of alignment. In many cases, your conference call can be replaced with an email, Slack message, or an @ mention in your team's project management software.

However, if your team struggles with writing clearly, start with small adjustments to give them time to learn and adapt. Keep in mind that clear written communication is a sign of clarity of thought. Writing a detailed memo requires better thought and understanding of what is important and how things are related. When your team members have clarity of thought, it's easier to rally your team around a common goal.

***

Regularly scheduled meetings can help align your organization and reduce other, unnecessary meetings. Consistently re-evaluating your process and looking for ways to improve the efficiency of your meetings, will give you an insight into whether these strategies are working for you or not. One thing to remember: not all meetings are bad. It's just about figuring out which ones work for your team and eliminating the rest. In some cases, you must communicate face to face and in person.

How to effectively delegate?

Short Answer

Delegation is a vital management skill and to properly put it into practice a project manager should know when to delegate up and down, how to identify which tasks and activities can be delegated, and how to provide the delegated party with context, clear instructions, and precise desired outcome to ensure efficiency.

A PM should also provide resources and continuous support for the proper execution of the delegated tasks. The hardest part of delegation might be delegating authority and responsibility but it is mandatory. A project manager should also make sure to give credit when the delegated tasks are as done as per requirements.

Explanation

Unless you are planning to do all the work by yourself, project management involves a good deal of delegation. We delegate to ensure ownership and coverage for all the necessary work, and also to gain confidence that the applied resources will be adequate to complete the project.

Delegating might sound easy, but efficiently passing the baton requires a great deal of trust, communication, and coordination. Nonetheless, if you learn how to effectively delegate, everyone on your team wins as delegating empowers your team, builds trust, and assists with professional development. Here are five key steps to start delegating more effectively.

1. Delegating up and down

Project management is a full-time job, so it is risky to retain ownership of too many scheduled project activities yourself. You should seek named owners other than yourself for all project tasks, even if you suspect that you will ultimately have to assist in bringing some of them to closure.

There is a wide range of responsibilities related to project management processes to account for. Normally, you will do most of the communication and reporting for your project, lead most of the meetings, and do other things that serve as the "glue" to hold your project together. That said, there can be situations where you may want to delegate some of this to others.

If there are technical complexities beyond your understanding, you may also need to delegate parts of the project definition and documentation to appropriate subject matter experts. A few years ago, I managed an IT security project, and since I was not a subject-matter expert at the time, I delegated almost everything involving technical work, and the project was a stunning success.

Unlike the downward delegation, upward delegation involves situations where you lack sufficient authority to proceed. Decisions involving significant amounts of money, life-cycle review approvals, or other aspects of project work beyond your control are often "kicked upstairs." Escalations of problems you are unable to resolve at your level of the organization are other frequent examples.

When you do have to delegate work upward, strive to appear as competent and professional as possible, and do it only when it is really necessary: Create a presentation or prepare a document that clearly summarizes the facts at hand, sets a clear deadline for resolution, and provides your thoughts or recommendations on the matter.

2. Knowing what and when to delegate

Another typical obstacle to delegation is that you might not be sure which tasks you should or shouldn't delegate. In every managers' workload, particularly new managers, there are undoubtedly certain tasks that they should personally undertake and other tasks that they should definitely consider delegating.

We recommend assessing your tasks by using the following rules to determine what tasks you should delegate:

- **Tiny tasks** are small chores that only take a short period of time to complete but usually add up over time. These might be things an assistant could do such as scheduling meetings, booking flights for business trips, or writing emails.
- **Tedious tasks** are mindless tasks, like copying and pasting data from your marketing automation tool to your CRM for instance. Such tasks require minimal skills and should be delegated too.

- **Teachable tasks** are time-consuming tasks that you can teach somebody else to complete. If a task does not require expertise that only you can provide, it's suitable for delegation.
- **Tasks that you are not so good at** that require a special set of skills, such as design for instance, where it would probably take you double the time to accomplish the task compared to a professional designer. In this case, it's better to delegate these tasks to someone who's equipped to do the work better and quicker.

Keep in mind that not every task can be delegated. For instance, performance reviews should be conducted by you. You can delegate information collection and analysis, but you cannot delegate discussing results with your team.

To conclude, is there a task you regularly tackle despite knowing your co-worker is better equipped to complete it? Would assigning the project tasks to other employees help them bolster their careers? If there's someone who could do the work better, or you think this could be a teachable moment: Delegate! It will show that you trust and value your team, while also giving you time to focus on more strategic projects.

3. Providing context, instructions, and feedback

When delegating a task to someone out of the blue, it is highly recommended to provide context for why you are entrusting them with this responsibility. When you choose someone to delegate to, explain why you chose them in particular and how you expect this to help them grow. This will allow them to consider each delegated task as a chance to take on more responsibilities or learn new skills.

When delegating, you should communicate to your employees the goals or milestones you hope to achieve and then let them tackle the problem in their own way. Don't look for perfection or incline to micromanaging; someone else can complete a task differently than you would. As long as you eventually get the desired outcome, the method shouldn't matter. According to the author of *The 7 Habits of Highly Effective People;* Stephen Covey, you should delegate results rather than methods: "For example, say, 'Here's what we are doing. Here's what we're after. I want you to get the sale,' instead of 'Follow up on those leads.'"

While you want to avoid micromanaging, you do want to establish a communication channel so that the person you're delegating to feels comfortable asking questions and providing progress updates. You've got to have a method to keep an eye on the progress along the way without getting in your employee's way. Setting up regular check-ins and providing feedback throughout the project can help with this.

When the work you delegated to your staff is complete, check that they did it correctly, and provide them with any needed feedback to better handle the task in the future.

4. Providing resources, authority, and support

When delegating, you must ensure that the tasked person has the needed skills to execute the delegated tasks successfully. A good training rule of thumb is 'I do, we do, you do' (i.e. watch me do this, then let's do it together, now you try). For instance, if you ask someone to accomplish a task with a tool they've never used before, make sure to help them get acquainted with it beforehand. If the individual to whom you are delegating work requires specific training or resources in order to execute the assigned work, it's your responsibility as a manager to provide both.

Setting someone up for a task without the needed resources will frustrate both parties; your employee will be unable to reach the intended outcome, and you will most likely need to put that work back on your to-do list.

Moreover, you need to allow for failure, not because your employees might fail, but because it will enable experimentation and empower the people you're assigning tasks to, to test new ideas and take a better approach. Remember that there's nothing worse than a manager delegating a task to a team member and then blaming them when anything goes wrong. Don't be that manager!

Delegating tasks without delegating any responsibility or authority is simply dumping on people. An effective delegation consists of assigning responsibility for results as well as the authority to do whatever is necessary to achieve the required outcomes. Delegating responsibility sends a strong message to your employees about how much you trust them and how competent and valuable they are to the organization.

Ultimately, you should support your employee through the execution phase of the delegated task regardless of whether or not they were able to attain the targeted outcome. Support should be majorly provided in failure since your employee would develop a fear of trying to handle new tasks in case you didn't show any support and guidance while delegating.

5. Giving credit

When someone accomplishes a task or project you delegated to them, you should express your gratitude and appreciation and point out particular details you think they performed well. When you notice those specifics, you're providing your employees with a roadmap for what they should continue to do to be successful. This might be the simplest step but it's one of the most difficult for many people to actually apply. Giving credit inspires loyalty, generates genuine satisfaction from the accomplished work and serves as a foundation for mentorship and performance evaluations.

After you've delegated tasks and they've been seen through to completion, you should credit and recognize that success because not only was the delegated task done the right way, but also this has the added benefit of making those around you more engaged. The more you thank and credit those you've delegated work to, the more likely it is they will want to help you on other projects in the future.

***

Delegating is a skill that must be practiced and refined over time. However, the better you get at matching the right people with suitable tasks and responsibilities, the more efficient you'll become at your job as a project manager. When you delegate effectively, you increase trust and dedication among employees, boost productivity, and ensure that all individuals are undertaking the tasks that are most suited to their skills and abilities. Thus, don't be hesitant to hand off the baton. It may take some practice at first to become an efficient delegator, but with some effort, you'll all go far.

How to deal with a team member who keeps missing deadlines?

Short Answer

Managing staff members who constantly fail to meet deadlines can be tedious and frustrating. So, what can you do about that? Well, you can start by establishing clear expectations and involve the employee in determining deadlines so they can be held responsible. Next, you must follow up by monitoring the work progress and measuring performance to solve any blockers the employee might face. When noticing a bad performance, you should sit down with the team member, ask what is going on, and provide support for them to reach better performance by explaining the impact of missing the deadlines on the project.

Explanation

Most project managers will admit that managing team members who keep missing deadlines is one of the least favorite parts of their job. Everyone is busy, and chasing after a poor performer is a waste of everyone's time. Managing a person who doesn't meet deadlines can be irritating, draining, and simply unpleasant. So, here are some things you can do to help you address this issue.

1. Setting clear expectations

When facing this kind of issue with one of your team members, you should clearly state your expectations for what needs to change going forward. Often this won't just mean "meet all deadlines". In some projects, especially those with heavy workloads and competing priorities, it might mean "come talk to me well in advance if something is getting in the way of you meeting the deadline."

In this context, what you want is both a heads-up and an opportunity to help move other priorities around. If your team member wasn't able to meet set deadlines, talk about the next steps. You want them to have a clear sense of what specific actions they will have to take to solve the problem, something more than just saying "Try harder."

Ideally, they should come up with these on their own, but if they're struggling, it's okay for you to be fairly direct about what you'd like them to try. When you set clear expectations, the employee not only understands the situation but they're also involved in establishing the deadline.

When you give a team member directives, ask them, "when do you think you can reasonably accomplish this task? " and allow them, within reason, to determine their deadlines, then hold them to it. This approach gives them an opportunity to think through what needs to be done and how long it would reasonably take them to complete the directive. When team members are involved in deciding how the task should be completed, it puts the responsibility and burden of meeting the setup goal on them while taking away the project manager's perception of setting up unrealistic expectations.

2. Monitoring progress and performance

Many project managers make the mistake of not following up with their team members about the assigned tasks. It is your role to check up on them to ensure that they have the resources they need to fulfill their job and also help them identify and address any barriers to completing their assignment.

Often, the ability to complete goals or job tasks is dependent on other people or departments. A great project manager is the one who helps their team navigate through those constraints. For instance, suppose an employee wants to conduct an audit and create a report on supply costs, but the accounting department refuses to give them the needed information to draft that report. This will impact the employee's ability to finish the audit before the pre-set deadline.

To avoid waiting until the last moment for your employee to notify you that they're not delivering what you're expecting on time, set a more frequent update schedule. You want to receive a current status update every few hours, days, or whatever you find suitable. You may need to remind the person to deliver their status update, but hopefully, they will do this on their own. If not, you may have a problem somewhere else, such as the discussed team member's basic work organization.

3. Communicating and providing support

Now that your team member has already missed the deadline, sit down with them and ask what's going on, and listen with an open mind. Start out by simply naming the problem and asking for their perspective: "You've been missing deadlines lately. What's been happening?" Then, give them some room to explain.

You might learn that deadlines haven't been as clear as you thought, or that someone else is causing a roadblock in their work. If you have trouble getting an understanding of what's causing the problem, try digging in a bit by asking questions like, "What's involved in making this happen?" and "What sorts of things are getting in the way?"

It is easy to forget about the details of some of these conversations that you have with your team members on a daily basis. So, make sure to take note of any discussion involving instructions, clarification, or task reminders. You don't have to write all of the discussion's details, simply write down the date, time, and summary of what you talked about. It is invaluable to have a file containing such details as a reminder for those rare occasions when a team member "forgets" specific directives. These notes are also helpful at performance appraisal time when assessing employee performance.

4. Clarify the impact of missed deadlines

When discussing missed deadlines with your team member, explain the impact of this issue. The idea here is to clarify that these aren't simply arbitrary deadlines; they have real-world implications when they're missed. For instance, you might say: "When you delivered your billings so late, your colleague ended up having to work over the weekend to get invoices out on time." Or, "We agreed that I'd be able to look at the brochure three days before it was due to the printer, but I received it too close to the print deadline to be able to give any meaningful feedback."

***

Team members who repeatedly fail to meet deadlines are detrimental to the health of your team and project, and even to organizational success. The only way to solve this problem is to address it straight up. If you want to avoid low individual morale, increased staff turnover, and poor project performance, you need to overcome your own distaste for uncomfortable confrontational discussions and offer your team the needed feedback to reach their best performance.

How to handle staff turnover?

Short Answer

First things first, not all turnover is bad. You might lose people who just don't belong to the organization's work culture and values. But, when you do lose valuable members you should be able to manage such turnover. To do that, start by analyzing the turnover by calculating the rate, costs, etc., and getting feedback to figure out the reasons, and accordingly implement an effective retention policy. Setting clear career paths, providing self-development and growth opportunities, avoiding micromanagement, and showing leadership can avert losing valuable resources.

Explanation

Staff turnover has a major impact on both your project and your organization's trajectory, but if you're having trouble with it, you're not alone. Even the best companies struggle with turnover. Every time a team member quits, it costs you to replace them and it disturbs your team. That's why it's critical to consider how to manage and minimize employee turnover.

You can't do much about people retiring or moving to a different city. However, you can stop them from leaving if they believe that they're underpaid or that they're not advancing career-wise. All you have to do is to give them a reason to stay. Consider the following steps to help reduce employee turnover and to ensure your key resources retention.

1. Analyzing the turnover

It's hard to change what you're not measuring. Upon unexpected employee turnover, It's important to collect the data carefully, understand that all turnover isn't equal and that how you measure employee turnover makes a difference.

There is a multitude of reasons people leave a job, and it's important not to lump all employee turnover into the same category. That is why you must measure your company turnover and culture. Once you've measured the turnover rate, you'll also want to measure the cost of employee turnover.

Along with measuring turnover rate, consider proactively soliciting feedback from team members before they leave. Quitting a job is a big decision, and it's not one that most people take lightly. When members of the team leave, how confident are you in your knowledge of why they left? Remember that gathering qualitative data through engagement surveys and other means is important.

Apart from conducting exit interviews, interviewing candidates carefully when recruiting, not just to ensure they have the right technical skills, but that they are also a cultural fit for the team and organization, is a key element of staff retention. Look at how you recruit new members of staff and ask yourself whether you see them working for you in a year's time. If you don't, make an effort to look for flexible staff who can adapt to your business needs. To further ensure successful recruitment, have multiple people interview the candidate. You will receive multiple perspectives and more people will feel committed to the new hire's success.

2. Putting people first

More than ever before, today's workforce values a blend between work and life. You should understand how important it is to acknowledge your people as unique contributors and value their time away from work. Fostering flexible schedules, for instance, is a way of putting people first. When possible, provide a compensatory time off after an extensive project. Try to promote a happy, productive, stress-free environment that acknowledges the fact that your team members have a life beyond work.

Make it a daily priority to check up on your team members, regularly ask how they're doing, and let them know how much you appreciate them. Be visible, approachable, and reachable. Consider, at least annually, reviewing reward and benefit programs to ensure competitiveness and alignment with employees' real requirements. This should cover not only basic and variable pay scales, but also long-term incentives, bonuses, and gain-sharing plans, along with health and wellness benefits.

A crucial factor to promote your team's well-being is their professional growth. Providing training will lead to a win-win situation for everyone. It won't only make your team more proficient and effective, but it will also lead to fewer feelings of stagnation and frustration which will eventually mold a more committed workforce. Investment in training is an investment in your team's future as it proves your long-term interest in them.

Along with providing training resources and learning experiences to help people grow and learn, focus on keeping the tempo up. Get to know what type of work excites particular team members, give them more opportunities to do challenging work, delegate something meaningful, and involve them in determining their vision and goals.

In my first job involving setting up a value-added service within a telecom operator, I quitted after two and half years. The main project I was working on went into maintenance and my role became limited to listening to the customer feedback and collaborating with the service provider. As you might guess, that was neither fulfilling nor exciting for me.

***

Employee turnover is a common issue for many projects, but it doesn't have to be for yours. It's one thing to say you're dedicated to building a strong culture or say that your team is your greatest asset, but are you genuinely following through on that rhetoric? Regularly reinforcing the value you place on your team's contributions and their happiness is one of the best ways to improve their experience at work and help you stay ahead of turnover.

How to deal with out-of-scope requests?

Short Answer

Out-of-scope requests or as it's called scope creep are a threat to any project. Understanding your client's vision and setting a clearly defined scope can prevent such an issue. If out-of-scope requests were made despite the above precautions, you should be clear with the client by referring back to the scope to remind them of the agreed-on project requirements and be bold when you take your decision to either refuse or accept the new requests. In case you accept the new requests under the frame of providing good customer service, try to manage this change effectively.

Explanation

Scope creep is when a client makes a request for work that goes beyond what was originally agreed upon. Scope creep happens when new tasks sneak up on you without being part of the Statement of Work (SOW). Ask any project manager, and the majority will tell you what a nightmare scope creep can be. You find yourself in the middle of the project, completely overwhelmed by the copious amount of client requests: It feels like you're drowning, and the entire project is sinking along with you.

In the midst of your despair, there's some good news: you can actually deal with scope creep. The next four steps will help you build a process that will enable you to handle scope creep while providing top-quality service for the client in terms of responding to their needs and providing satisfactory solutions.

1. Be clear and bold

As the project manager, it is your responsibility to state clearly what is included in the scope and what is out of scope. The client may not know everything it takes for you to complete your work promptly. What may seem to be a "small change" to them may be a complex mess to you.

If a client asks for something out of scope, alert them to this immediately. For example, you can just say: "I can definitely take care of that for you. However, that is outside of the scope written in our agreement, and this new request may change the project deadline. Do you want to rescope the project and budget or save the change until the project is complete?"

At this point, it is up to the client to choose if they want to re-scope the project or not, either way, the choice is theirs. Make sure to clearly explain to your client the process of adding new tasks to the project. Always keep a close eye on the project timeline, budget, and capacity of your resources.

Often, clients will keep making requests until you say no. Can you really blame them? Who wouldn't want to get every ounce of work they can for the money? That's why project management requires such diligence. If you're diligent, it may mean that you find yourself saying no more than you'd like, and you might hate saying no.

So, instead of a downright refusal, you might consider taking a roundabout approach to scope creep which looks something like this: "Our current agreement is for [current terms] at [agreed budget]. From what you shared, you'd like to add [scope creep request]... I'd be willing to do that for [new budget and schedule based on additional request]. Or if that's outside your budget, we can just stick to our original terms." This will set clear expectations of what delivering scope creep might require.

Ultimately, in order to prevent this situation, you should establish two-way communication to regularly communicate with your clients so that both parties are fully aware of what to expect from each other. A communication gap between clients and project managers usually leads to scope creep, which could push a project towards failure.

2. Refer to the project scope

A statement of work is the part of the client agreement that would outline all of the work that you are going to do. Other than the area in which you discuss payment, the statement of work is one of the most important parts of a client agreement. The SOW should clearly, always clearly, define the milestones and tasks of the project, and how the deliverable should be used by the end-user.

SOW
Table of
Content

1. Signature
2. Introduction
3. Project Scope
4. Out of Scope
5. Software Bill of Materials
6. Deliverables
7. Assumptions
8. Implementation schedule
9. Project commercials
10. Payment schedule
11. Expiration

Statement of Work (SOW) elements

Additionally, if needed, define any limitations that may affect the project scope since scope creep does not necessarily come from outside; it may as well stem from the goodwill of your team members. Your team members hopefully want to deliver their best, but sometimes that might be reaching too far out of scope. Ultimately, putting profitability and the time frame at risk.

At the beginning of each project, take time to outline requirements and clarify goals and objectives. The initial planning stage will save you from a huge headache down the road. Unfortunately, sometimes, and despite your efforts to outline everything, scope creep still happens. And when it happens, it's easiest to simply point clients to the documented project requirements.

Here is a sample script for this situation: "We're glad you're so excited about what we're achieving that you want to add more. Unfortunately, your request falls out of the scope of our initial project outline. For your convenience, I've attached the project requirements to this email. Should we discuss expanding the budget and project scope? I'd be happy to meet with you later this week."

When the client inevitably makes out-of-scope requests, don't be shy about telling them that it's not part of what you agreed on, and that showing flexibility on your part by accepting such additional requirements might require flexibility from their part cost and time-wise.

3. Good customer service

As you gain more experience with certain types of projects, you'll be able to determine the common things people tend to request. To this point, there are times in which clients will ask for things you did not initially agree upon, and it would be a great customer service move to do the work for them to build trust.

However, if you do choose to complete extra work that wasn't agreed upon, make sure you get credit for it. This approach not only sets an expectation but shows that you want to invest in them. Yet, you should be careful; don't approve extra work without going back to your line manager. If you don't, you will be later questioned why it was added to the project.

When I managed a value-added service in the telecommunication industry my project got around eight change requests in the span of two years. Usually, when the customer approaches me for a change my answer is "We can do it, but let me first check with my team". After a few days, I send the technical document of change and ask if they want to proceed. In that case, I involve the sales team and send them an offer.

4. Manage change effectively

When you are managing a dynamic project, effective change management is crucial for success. When a client comes to you with a scope change request. Instead of feeling the pressure of making a yes or no decision on the spot, use something like this instead:
"Thanks for sharing this great idea. I can see why you'd like to add it to the project. Something of this magnitude needs to get the approval of our project sponsor, though. I'll need to pitch the idea to him. Please shoot me an email back with the following information: the new functionality, the business value of the change, and any consequences that could occur if we don't make the change."

Be clear with the client on what the plan of attack is for amendments before anything happens. Explain how change requests are submitted, who is in charge of them, how they get handled in terms of budget and timeline, and what their implications are for the project as a whole. Having everything out in the open from the very beginning will enable you to manage your client's expectations effectively and keep the project on track.

***

To protect your project from scope creep, make sure you understand the needs of your client. Ensure you have the same view of the scope, the vision, and the project altogether. All stakeholders, your team, and your client need to be on the same page initially and as the project progresses.

Overcoming the scope creep problem is not as difficult as many people initially think. With few adjustments to your approach, you can achieve better results. Effective change management, regular communication, and collaboration with clients, as well as continuously iterating and learning will resolve most of your scope creep issues.

If you are managing a project with a lot of uncertainty, then you can follow the Agile approach for a more flexible scope. This will be examined more in detail in the last chapter of the book addressing Agile.

How to handle a team member's bad attitude or behavior?

Short Answer

Handling a stakeholder's bad attitude and negativity is one of the trickiest tasks of being a project manager but it's essential. You may want to start with open communication to understand what's going on and assess the situation. Once you become aware of the problem, reach out to the concerned person to explain the situation, the behavior, and the impact it has on the work environment.

Next, you should observe the stakeholder for any behavior changes. If the bad attitude still continues, you should call it out immediately when you spot it without making it look like a personal attack. Still, if you discussed the matter again with nothing changing, you may want to consider letting them go.

Explanation

Team members with bad attitudes can be deeply destructive to any project. Even the smallest aspects of toxic behavior can cause a major negative impact including customer loss, team demotivation and demoralization, increased turnover, and loss of legitimacy among important external stakeholders.

In such situations, you may find it easier to turn a blind eye to the issue instead of choosing confrontation. It's normal to feel uncomfortable about confronting such an issue. However, you can't let this go on without treating it. When someone is toxic, negative, or has any type of bad behavior, you should try to understand what they need or why they are acting this way.

Through the next steps, you will be able to learn how to properly and efficiently deal with bad behavior in the workplace.

1. Open communication

Often, you won't know about someone's negativity unless it is brought to your attention, since team members with negative attitudes will surely behave differently around you. The solution for this issue starts with establishing open communication with your entire team. You want everyone to know that if a problem occurs, you're always ready to hear it.

In order to decrease the distance between you and your team, make an effort to understand their point of view. Just sit and listen to what your stakeholders are experiencing. You may learn why they're acting the way they do.

2. Assessing the situation

Don't rush to judgment and criticism, saying things like "You're too negative" as it may prove to be useless. Instead, try to provide three key pieces of information to the individual in question: the situation, behavior, and impact.

For instance, explain to them that in meetings (the situation), their comments and questions tend to be always negative (the behavior) and that this kind of action will make it harder for them to build relationships and be successful in the organization (the impact). Finish up by saying something like, "I trust that you know we want you to be successful here. So, how can we best assist you in overcoming this in the future?"

By focusing your intervention this way, you are attempting to prevent the impression that it's a personal attack. Make it clear that it's never personal. Finally, you should give the team member a chance to respond. Next, observe their actions and change course if necessary.

3. Calling out bad behavior

In some cases, after talking with the person in question, they might express their intent to change their attitude. But, in other cases, and even when your team member says that they do want to improve their attitudes, they may be so used to negativity that they don't realize they're still acting the same way. So it's important to point out these behaviors as soon as they reappear again.

Calling out bad behavior when witnessed will probably make this person try harder to reduce their negativity and improve their behavior. The right step to take is to start to name the blaming behavior when it occurs. For example, when one team member starts to speak harshly about another person, call their attention to it. "It seems like you're being pretty harsh on "A". I don't think it's helpful. Could you please try being a bit more positive about it?"

You're probably thinking that this is going to annoy people. Yes, you're right. It probably will. However, this is necessary to help people understand that their behavior is being noticed and refused.

Unless you highlight the unwanted behavior, the member will continue to act the way they always have and then, you'll have yourself to blame. Don't be fooled though, this technique won't solve the problem by itself. It may simply drive the behavior underground. In other words, your team member may just wait until you're out of sight before acting as they usually do.

4. When to take action

When naming the bad behavior that isn't working, you should think about the role that these people play in your project. Are they actually a liability? Can they be repurposed to fulfill another role? One thing is for sure, you cannot tolerate team members who are a bad influence on others by spreading their bad attitude.

Sometimes, the person simply isn't a good cultural fit when they show they can't or won't change, so it's time to just let them go. It's critical to take action promptly before they deteriorate the team from within: Toxic team members easily corrupt their coworkers.

You might ask: What if this person is an outstanding, skilled team member? Still, it's not worth the risk of keeping them around. In fact, their negativity will most likely end up decreasing their productivity anyway. Negative-minded team members are more prone to get mentally weary and defensive, which ultimately results in a decline in production.

None of this suggests that workplace criticism is a bad thing. Constructive criticism is an important aspect of every successful company. The key is for any criticism to serve as part of a positive effort to help the organization move forward, and more importantly to be presented with respect and appreciation.

***

Don't let an individual's bad attitude in the workplace ruin your team relationships and productivity. Letting it spiral out of control will simply cause issues in the long term and distract your team from its true purpose of ensuring the project's success. Name the bad behavior, make an effort to understand the other side, and shut down continuing negativity. Your team will thank you for it.

How to recover a troubled project?

Short Answer

Recovering a troubled project is a challenging task that requires specific attention, management, and leadership skills to successfully save the project from failing. Finding a solution lies in finding the reason why the project went off rails in the first place.

After identifying root causes, you should assess the situation to get a full picture of the process, people, and product dimensions of the project. Next, you must set up a recovery plan including new priorities, objectives, potential work, etc., all of which will be implemented and monitored to ensure recovery.

Explanation

A troubled project is one in which the gap between what is expected and what is delivered surpasses the acceptable tolerance limits, pushing it down a path that will inevitably lead to failure. Therefore, a special effort is required to either define a recovery plan or decide on early termination, as both choices are considered as ways to handle troubled projects.

However, not every issue that arises in a project is deemed significant enough for the project to be considered troubled. For instance, a three-year project that is scheduled to be completed a week late is not a troubled project. Therefore, it is very important to understand the acceptable tolerance limit because the project may be over-budget or overdue but still in an acceptable range, although those might be early warning signs of a troubled project.

Often, project managers have an ambiguous attitude toward a troubled project. On one hand and on a personal level, a troubled project is demanding, with unfulfilled expectations, pressure, conflict, and hard work. On the other hand, it requires practicing the best of project management: establishing direction, prioritizing issues, gathering people around a common objective, negotiating objectives, and solving problems.

Here, I am explaining the approach for identifying and dealing with troubled projects with confidence and control. We will go through four critical steps to recovery, highlighting the major activities and actions necessary for turning a failing project into a success.

1. Understanding the roots of trouble

Troubled projects are often the result of poor project management processes or poor process implementations. But, following good project management practices does not guarantee project success. People or product-related problems, like team knowledge, project management experience, and solution complexity might also compromise the project outcome. At the organizational level, factors like management and user support can also influence project success. Outside the organization, market and economic context may lead to frequent changes or impose budget and time constraints that can put the project in peril.

Typically, on a troubled project, there isn't just one problem, but several underlying problems. These problems tend to be complicated, multidisciplinary, and interconnected. For example, changing scope without increasing the budget and extending the schedule will add more work on a limited period of time and amount of resources leading to an increase in product defects.

Mainly, to identify a troubled project's root causes, you will need to gather data on time, cost, and scope and compare actual performance to estimates, which will usually reveal variances. But, not all variances are automatically considered red flags. The problem in effect occurs when those variances greatly exceed "acceptable" levels that attention must be paid to making the necessary corrections in order to bring the project in line with the expected baseline performance.

Numerous case studies have demonstrated that projects almost always become troubled toward the end of the project life cycle. Thus, the crisis occurs near the point at which the project should be close to full-scale implementation. Obviously, this is the most inconvenient time for things to go wrong.

It's important to note that project monitoring and control are only part of the process of assessing whether or not a project is "troubled". Keeping an eye on the human element will also reveal important information about the real status of a project.

2. Planning the rescue process

When a recovery strategy for a project is prepared, it's important to know what primarily drove the project to its current status. Obviously, if the drivers are not eliminated, the project might be recovered in the short term, but with time it can fall back into the same critical stage it was in before the recovery process.

Recovering a project entails saving losses, restoring the project's usefulness, and preventing its total failure. Basically, recovery involves readjusting the fundamentals of the project's scope, schedule, and budget, which are methodologically referred to as the project's triple constraint, as well as its resources. This can be done through multiple options depending on the specific issues the project is facing.

One recovery option is by reducing the project scope, maintaining the planned budget and schedule. This process can save parts of the project that may survive without full scope.

You can also work on maintaining project scope, inflating project costs, and maintaining the planned schedule. Usually, this process is used when project scope cannot be reduced and the interest in results outweighs the shortfall caused by an increase in costs. Maintaining project scope by extending project deadlines and the budget forecast is another way to recover your troubled project. This is usually used when the schedule is not critical for the project, where a slowdown may avoid an increase in cost, thus allowing you to maintain the scope.

These options are the foundations for any type of recovery. All other types and solutions proposed are but variations resulting from one of these options. In addition to this resizing of the triple constraint, several other factors could help. For instance, having a supportive sponsor will send a reassuring message to all stakeholders that the project will recover.

3. Implementing and controlling the rescue process

With a revised scope, schedule, and budget it's now time to implement remedial actions and start making progress. During the intervention phase, you should regularly collect work performance information, update micro and macro plans, maintain the project documents, analyze project metrics, and report performance.

Collecting work performance information should be a frequent routine since it is critical for a project rescue process. Work performance information can include the start and finish status of scheduled activities, estimated completion dates, actual and remaining work, resources used, and percentage of completion.

To gather work performance information the project can combine frequent face-to-face meetings or at least live distance meetings, frequent on-the-job reviews, and collaboration tools to collect status information and update project documents.

Additionally, the micro plan should be updated daily, recording actual and remaining values. Future activities, estimates, and sequences are permanently reviewed to ensure a high level of detail. Also, the macro plan can be regularly updated using the information on the micro plans and available resource capacity.

Analyzing metrics during this phase is essential. Metrics that can be used to monitor the rescue process include the number of open problems, risks, and defects organized by priority, schedule variance expressed in days or percentage, work variance expressed in hours or percentage, a cumulative slip which is the sum of variances in days between schedule and actual finish dates, earned value management metrics, and more.

Once the rescue is complete, you should hold a "lessons learned" meeting with the project team and key stakeholders to discuss what went well, and what could have been improved on the rescue process.

***

When you are about to recover a troubled project, make sure that you approach the project correctly. Most importantly, do not forget what the actual goal of the project initially was. Make sure that the business case is sound, and only then pursue the project objectives and recover the project.

IV. Technical skills

Project management might be the only profession where technical, business, and soft skills routinely intersect.

Technical skills are a must-have for project managers to become successful. You must be fully proficient with the tools and techniques of the trade. While you don't necessarily need to be a domain expert, which is a common misconception when we're talking about technical skills, you do need basic familiarity and top view knowledge of the field you are in. Gaining some technical expertise as a novice project manager can vastly help your team build higher-quality deliverables for your clients.

In this book section, we're going to identify what technical skills will be handy when leading your project, how to understand and familiarize yourself with the technical work done by your team so that you can do your own job as a project manager better, and how to not get overwhelmed by technical issues you might run across.

How to efficiently frame and meet your client's expectations?

Short Answer

Meeting your client expectations is crucial to keep them invested in you and your project. In order to meet those expectations, you must frame them first. Setting clear deliverables from the beginning and investigating feasibility will lead to setting realistic expectations.

Those deliverables and expectations should be documented under the project scope to avoid any future misunderstanding or out-of-scope requests. You should mainly be transparent and honest with your client in order to build a strong relationship. Regular communication and feedback will be your tool to improve and meet or even go beyond expectations.

Explanation

Working with a new client is always stressful. You have to really get to know your customer to figure out what their expectations are early on. Here are some tips to help you frame and meet your client expectations both in terms of investment performance and your service quality.

1. Set clear deliverables and realistic expectations

Sometimes a client's expectations may not be feasible and you should let them know that. Overpromising is a big mistake when it comes to managing clients' expectations. Only promise what you can deliver, then there will be no place for dissatisfaction later on.

How well you manage expectations depends majorly on your communication skills. So listen, be proactive, address issues directly, don't hesitate to ask follow-up questions in case of need, and you will be able to keep your client's expectations in check.

For instance, glitches, errors, and bugs occurring in software development can be irritating and costly to customers. However, clients will become angrier if they look forward to their problem being solved in a week, and instead wait two weeks. You can manage customer expectations by clearly stating how long it will take to address an issue from the moment it arises until it is resolved.

Teams should notify customers of how much time and effort will be required to come up with a solution as promptly as possible.

While optimism is essential for a positive customer experience, you must also be realistic when it comes to solutions. By grasping the company's policies, the complexities of certain issues, and the workload of your team members, you can determine how a particular ticket will be solved and the time investment it will require. While it can be nerve-wracking to tell a client a problem will take longer than expected to resolve, it is more important to be realistic than set expectations that can't be met.

2. Document scope clearly

Expectation setting is critical. It starts with asking the client what they're hoping to achieve and really driving at specifics. Ask them what success looks like and exhaust that line of discussion. Expectation setting is enhanced by in-person meetings where you can develop a closer connection and have a more meaningful dialogue with the client. Start your business relationship by organizing a kick-off meeting. This way, both the client and the team can set clear expectations on what the deliverables are and when to expect them.

A scope document is necessary to help both you and your client understand what to exactly expect throughout the course of the project. It's too late to start managing a client's expectations in the middle of delivering a service or a product. You must begin managing expectations right at the outset of the project in order to be effective.

It would be nice to be able to take the quickest and easiest path of just discussing work with a client and then get it done. The challenge is that people hear and interpret the same message in different ways.

To protect your client and yourself from any future misunderstanding, you can say: "This is what I heard you say, this is what I plan to do, and this is the cost of the effort." Making this statement forces you to consider the various aspects of the project or request, gives the client your interpretation of what they want you to accomplish, verifies the project's who, what, when, where, and how, and forces the client to validate your interpretation of the planned work.

The level of detail you put into a scope document will vary based on both the project and your client. In some cases, you might want to simply use a follow-up email to clarify what you're planning to do and include the scope document before you do any work.

Determine the level of description you need based on your client's need for details and the complexity of the project. If your work includes programming changes, include an application design or a system workflow that provides enough detail for the client to see and agree on the deliverable. For a Web site design, this might include a short written description as opposed to detailed Web page designs.

The scope should also include the project plan where you define the specifics of the work execution to a level of detail that helps the client understand what you're intending to do in the project and how the process will work. The plan needs to include key milestones and estimated time frames. You can also include resource needs, cost, and payment plan.

3. Be transparent and honest

Put yourself in your client's shoes and ask yourself how you would like to be treated, what do you appreciate in terms of service and how do you feel when someone doesn't meet your expectations?

Transparency is absolutely crucial to managing customer expectations effectively as it has a direct impact on the clients' ability to trust your organization. Regardless of the situation, you should avoid keeping secrets at all costs. Be clear with clients about what they are going to receive. This is something that can be done when you review the signing contract. A clear itemized list will provide a great deal of clarity. The most important thing is, to be honest from the beginning.

4. Establish regular communication

Lack of communication is usually at the root of all issues, and your relationship will suffer if you don't start being proactive about communication when it comes to both good and bad news.

When you encounter underperformance, for instance, own it and control your reaction. Clients will follow where you lead them and they will put the focus where you do. So, try to put the poor performance into perspective.

You should work on building a strong relationship that goes beyond the client/project manager dynamic. People do business with people they like and trust, so you need to develop a personal relationship with your clients. A great deal of managing expectations relies on this.

To establish yourself early on as a valuable resource, make sure to maintain regular communication, get to know your clients well, try to understand what makes them tick, and translate that into the relationship.

Clients may be unsure of what they want to achieve or they may not articulate it properly so develop excellent listening skills so you can identify their messages by asking relevant questions to help you grasp both your client's conscious and unconscious beliefs and expectations.

It's your job as the project manager to set clear boundaries and expectations about your commitment to the project and the people involved, so they can feel safe and supported rather than overwhelmed. To do that, it's recommended to send a welcome email with a warm and relaxed tone to communicate trust and support.

***

The first step to delivering excellence is to manage expectations effectively from the get-go. You might be in for a bumpy ride if you skip any of the steps above with your client. Having these discussions with your client before you start working will allow your project to run smoothly and help everyone reach what they hoped for.

How to accurately estimate project cost and duration?

Short Answer

You need to be well acquainted with your project's team, deliverables, activities, and processes in order to be able to produce precise and accurate budget and schedule estimations. Start by gathering data samples of similar past projects to get a better sense of your project's overall needed level of effort and costs.

Identifying and allocating resources to tasks based on their capacities and skills is also key for estimation accuracy. Opting for a process or approach you actually understand and master will further improve your estimations. Verifying, controlling, and making some improvements depending on the project's live performance is mandatory.

Explanation

Estimating the duration and budget of your project can be a challenging task regardless of the project size. To generate a workable, accurate estimate, you must be acquainted with every detail concerning your team and your project deliverables, tasks, and processes. You must also be ready to approach your client to ask whatever questions you think will help you get any useful details for the estimation process.

Every client has a specific budget in mind, thus they want to know the costs before they're willing to begin a project. Inaccurate project estimation can lead to problematic outcomes since it limits profits, impairs quality, drains your team, impedes development, and blunts your competitive edge.

However, you don't need the extra expenses of heavy-duty project management tools to improve your project planning. We're going to break down the only steps you need to take in order to master projects' estimation.

1. Understanding requirements

Whether you're estimating a project based on a Request for Proposal (RFP), a discussion, or a concisely written email, you must understand every detail of the project in order to be able to provide an accurate realistic estimation. This usually necessitates thorough inquiry. By asking questions, you will be able to produce your project estimate based on what your clients actually require rather than what you believe they need.

When trying to accurately estimate your project's time and budget, consider the following: What is the project goal? How will you and your client judge whether or not the project is successful? What deliverables will you and your client set as the project outcome? What range of services does the project require? What is your client's budget for the project? Is there technology involved? If yes, what is the technology? Is your client employing someone who is knowledgeable about the topic? What is the timeline for the project, and will your client require your services after you complete the project work?

Depending on the level of information offered by your client, these questions can go on and on. You should be persistent in order to obtain all of the information and details you need. And, if your client is not inclined to answer a question, take a note. You may need it as proof later if an issue occurs.

Before estimating your project activities in a more detailed manner, a high-level estimate for the overall project is usually carried on by the project sponsor and stakeholders involved in the project initiation. These estimates may be based on some analysis, or they may be wild guesses pulled out of the air; whatever their basis, these initial estimates should be treated only as general goals.

Although they may also represent some known constraints, the initial top-down estimates can be used only as provisional starting points. Setting a realistic project baseline requires thorough planning, analysis, and precise estimations by the project team being responsible for executing work.

2. Relying on similar past project data

Obviously, each project is unique. Project managers come across a multitude of different clients, team members, technologies, communication tools, etc But, this does not mean that projects can't share some similarities.

Historical data can indisputably be a helpful reference when conducting your new projects' estimations. When referring back to any previous similar projects, you may end up finding some information, notes, or reports that can be useful for creating better and valid estimates. For instance, you can check the time your team members spent on similar tasks within antecedent projects to get a better sense of the required effort to accomplish your current project's work.

But, how do you actually get the historical data of past projects to estimate future ones? And how can you quickly and easily analyze it? While some project managers still opt for spreadsheets for project tracking, project management tools, such as JIRA, Asana, Monday, or Trello, allow you to capture every task you and your team perform on projects.

By using one of these tools, you can include all of the details and data your project is generating into simple dashboards and shareable reports. You'll also be able to effectively access and monitor how your project's time is being spent, allowing you to take proactive actions when needed to steer your project in the right direction.

3. Selecting estimation methods

Any project, without any exceptions, can be fragmented into phases, tasks, and subtasks. Upon breaking down the project, it will be much easier to first estimate each element's required execution time, and then map it all out to create an overall solid project time estimate.

The most accurate project planning and estimation method is the bottom-up technique which uses the Work Breakdown Structure (WBS). A WBS is a deliverable-oriented breakdown of a project into smaller components. It is composed of a hierarchy of specific elements, where an element can be a product, data, or service.

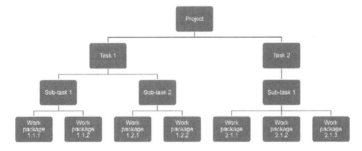

Work Breakdown Structure (WBS)

Other project estimation techniques include:

- **Expert judgment:** relies on the standpoint of an individual who typically owns enough knowledge and expertise to help you make the right estimations.
- **Comparative or analogous estimation:** relies on historical information to estimate current activities' durations. Analogous estimating is also known as top-down estimating.
- **Parametric model estimating:** uses a mathematical model to calculate how long an activity will take based on the "quantities" of work to be completed. For example, you can estimate completing 1 km of fencing in 10 days if your team is able to fence 100 meters per day.
- **Three-point estimating:** generates an average estimation based on pessimistic, optimistic, and "most likely" estimates.

4. Verifying estimates

Project estimates are predictive metrics, and because they are initially forecasts of the future, they tend to be somewhat imprecise. You can substantially improve their accuracy over time by collecting actual measurements at the end of completed projects. Such retrospective metrics provide feedback to improve your estimating processes and to increase the confidence of those involved in the estimation process.

At the activity level, the status you collect throughout the project will either confirm the predictions in your plans or clearly show where you were in error. There are many metrics useful for this, including actual activity durations, actual activity effort consumption, actual activity costs, number of added, unplanned activities, etc.

Unexpected staff turnover or adding staff can also lead to significant estimating problems because dealing with mid-project learning curve issues usually consumes substantial unplanned time and effort. Life-cycle measures are useful for spotting underestimates and missing work in project plans.

***

When examining the initial estimates, be skeptical of anything that appears either too conservative or too optimistic. Make sure to ask questions about the basis for the cost and duration estimates, and probe to uncover exactly how the work is to be done. An accurate project estimation will be your key to deliver your project on time and within budget.

How to operate a small project?

Short Answer
Small projects can actually benefit from the same kind of prioritization and planning that large projects require. The difference is that small projects don't really require a lot of planning. Fast-track planning can be enough to build the project structure and define objectives, scope, and deliverables. When opting for a methodology, choose one that focuses more on delivering rather than producing huge quantities of project documentation. Communication, tracking, and reporting still take place but on a smaller range.

Explanation
For less complicated projects, the overall project management process may be streamlined and simplified, but it still takes place. Planning, team building, implementing basic processes, and closing the project are all essential.

As an active project manager, I often get asked whether the best practices, tools, and approaches of project management are applicable for all projects regardless of their size. This is a really important question and the answer is "projects are not similar, so tailoring is a must". Let's then see how you can tailor your processes when it comes to small projects.

1. Defining objectives, scope, and deliverables

Even the smallest projects have objectives that must be attained. It is in your best interest as the project manager to identify these objectives since you will likely be assessed on whether or not the project reached them. Keep in mind that you still have to define and document these objectives even as long as you want to satisfy the needs of the stakeholders since that is what you are initially paid to do.

Somebody is going to have to carry out the actual work to produce whatever is delivered from your project. Even if the deliverables are relatively small, not requiring much time to accomplish, they should be documented. Your goal should be to provide a sufficiently elaborate description of the project deliverables. It is important to write down this description in a clear and straightforward manner even if it consists of one page.

When you don't document deliverables properly, people executing the project work can interpret what is required in unexpected ways which will only result in rework later on to correct mistakes. So, make sure to always define and document deliverables thoroughly and clearly.

The same goes with defining the scope. The scope represents the boundaries of your project. If you don't define it beforehand, it will expand and grow out of control as the project progresses, and while you might have started with a relatively small project before you realize it, your project will become bigger than you anticipated.

Moreover, even with a small project, you must document who the involved stakeholders are. By identifying and defining the project stakeholders from the beginning, you will make sure that you are covering all of their needs when defining the objectives and deliverables.

2. Fast-Track planning

Planning a small project can be simplified as you may not need any sophisticated project management scheduling software to document your project. With sufficiently straightforward projects, creating a simple spreadsheet can work as a planning tool. It is simple and more than adequate for small projects.

In addition to the activities list, you will have to document the milestones of the project and the responsibilities of each team member. Keep in mind that even the smallest projects require determining which activities are needed to generate a deliverable.

You should estimate how much time these activities will take, decide on the number of staff members, identify any other resources that the project will require, and finally assign activities and responsibilities to your staff. I usually recommend Google services like Drive to promote collaboration and ensure that documents can be accessed and used effectively by everyone involved.

3. Focusing on project delivery

One of the most used arguments against project management approaches is that they are highly process-centric leading to massive amounts of project documentation which are just not desirable nor practical when managing a small project.

Depending on your project type, you can opt for an agile method of development rather than the traditional waterfall approach, as agile methods' main focus is value delivery rather than documentation.

You may ask: How much documentation is really necessary? I strongly believe in only producing as much documentation as required by the project, nothing more and nothing less. A basic rule of thumb is, if it's useful in helping you deliver the business goals of the project then produce it, if it isn't useful in helping you deliver the business objectives of the project, then don't waste your time on it.

4. Communication, tracking, and reporting

Communication may also be minimal on simple projects, but you should plan for at least weekly status collection and reporting, as well as conducting short periodic team meetings throughout the project.

Even with the smallest project teams composed of just a Project Manager and another contributor, the project manager will still have to assign tasks and responsibilities to the other person. You can't assume that they will know what they should do without it being effectively communicated to them. If you don't allocate them some specific tasks, chances are they will probably work on other things that are not required. As a result, either the project will end up delivering inaccurate outcomes, or it will be delayed since you will have to eventually invest more time in tasks that should have been done in the first place.

Work monitoring may also be less formal on small projects, but still, you should collect and distribute status reports at least weekly in order to maintain effective ongoing communication with each project contributor. You should schedule and be disciplined about both one-on-one communication and periodic team meetings to keep things moving and under control. Overall, you should watch out for problems and difficulties, and adjust the processes you're using for your project to balance the trade-off between excessive overhead and insufficient control.

Ultimately, projects without elaborate, complex deliverables are generally not difficult to close. You should always conclude your project, no matter how small, simple, or brief it was, with a quick assessment of lessons learned to capture what went well and what should be changed in the future. Adjust the planning and other template information for use on future similar projects.

***

In conclusion, applying best practices to a small project can be accomplished without excessive paperwork or overhead. Best practices are processes, methods, and implementations that many project managers have used throughout numerous projects and that are considered to be "best practices" because they help you reach the best outcomes. You should not assume that just because you're managing a small project you can disregard such practices; if you do, you'll end up regretting it later on when your project turns into a mess.

When and how to hire a freelancer?

Short Answer

A project manager should start considering adding a freelancer to the team to deal with an unsteady workload. In case you need a rare set of skills for a specific mission, a freelancer could be the ideal option. You can also recruit a freelancer when you need immediate added value with no training required, or when you need a new fresh perspective and thought diversity. As to how to hire a freelancer, you should first determine the work scope and payment range, and then start your research on freelancing platforms or Facebook groups.

Explanation

Freelancers are independent workers who are usually highly skilled in a certain domain and conveniently available for on-demand work. Often, businesses opt for freelancers during periods of peak demand to expand their workforce, then revert back to a leaner team when the workload drops.

With so many talents opting for freelancing for a variety of reasons, it's only natural to consider the option of hiring one. If you have decided you need a freelancer but you're not sure where to start, don't worry. I will go through everything you need to know about when and how you can hire a freelancer.

1. When to hire a freelancer

Are you feeling overwhelmed at work and need more hands-on-deck? Or, are you considering expanding your team but you don't have enough budget to leverage? Hiring a freelancer might be the solution to your problem. We all need some kind of work done and sometimes, hiring a full-time staff member is not what you need. If you are not sure whether a full-time employee would make sense for you, a freelancer could definitely be a good option.

Usually, when the company is growing, the workload won't be stable. This is common for project-based businesses such as marketing and Public Relations agencies and software development companies. Hiring and relying on a pool of freelancers with whom they work on a regular basis enables such organizations to reduce costs and increase profit margins. With freelancers, you are able to quickly get high value and you can even use them in a more flexible way (i.e. more hours when you need them most and fewer hours during slower periods).

Apart from workload volatility, hiring freelancers allows you to have all the skills your project requires, whenever you need them. For example, imagine that you are implementing an ERP system and you need someone who has experience with a very similar project within the same industry. It is expected that the project will be completed in six months, therefore the person you will be hiring will not be needed afterward. Then, what options do you have? Hiring a full-timer and asking your company to find a different role for them once the project is over? Or outsourcing the project to a consulting company? Often, the best you can do is to hire a highly skilled freelancer on a project basis.

Finally, hiring individuals with different backgrounds, skills sets, and expertise brings value to the team. It appears that freelancers who worked with more than one client often bring a fresh perspective and may even help resolve a problem faster, as they are likely to have faced a similar challenge previously when working for another client. Working with a range of companies in different fields certainly allows them to learn some "tricks" from each gig. A freelancer's abilities and efficiency improve over time as they become a "Jack of all Trades."

2. How to hire a freelancer

Before you start searching for freelancers, you must determine exactly what needs to be done. If you want the best person for the job, you need to be crystal clear about the service they need to provide. Your job description needs to include every detail concerning the freelancer's mission.

Thoroughly consider what exactly needs to be done and put it all on paper. Who knows, maybe it winds up to be a reoccurring work and then you may need a full-time employee after all. A properly drafted job description and Scope Of Work (SOW) will ensure that you will secure the suitable person for the job since they will be able to know if they will be capable of fulfilling your requirements or not. This will also allow your potential freelancers to give you an accurate estimate of work duration, along with a specific price for the job. They will be able to deliver a better product because they have more instructions and they don't need to spend time asking questions and searching for more details.

Now it's time for you to decide how much you want to pay. Firstly, since many freelancers pay their own taxes and run their own businesses, their hourly and project rates are often higher than those of in-house staff. Secondly, a freelancer's location will also play a part in their pricing too. A freelancer from Vietnam and a freelancer from Canada for instance will certainly have different rates. Thirdly, there is the matter of experience. Someone who's just starting out will have wildly different rates from someone who has extensive experience. Therefore, you should expect to pay more for freelancers who are experts in the field, or those with specific experience in your niche.

Freelancers are charged either by the hour or by the overall result or final product and as a client, you must decide which approach would be more suitable and especially more cost-effective for you. For example, you should consider an hourly rate agreement if you only have a small writing task that might require a few hours to accomplish. But, for long-term projects, choosing a pay-per-result approach would make more sense.

Now, you'll have to face one of the most challenging aspects of hiring a freelancer; actually finding one. Thanks to the power of the Internet, it became seamless to find the perfect freelancer. One of the best sources to find qualified freelancers fast is Social media. Social media platforms such as Facebook, Reddit, and LinkedIn, are often excellent resources for finding qualified freelancers. Look for online forums and groups on Facebook and Reddit that are specially dedicated to freelancing job offers. You can either search by specialty field, such as "3D modeling freelancers" or "AutoCAD freelancers", or by country, such as "Freelancers in India".

Another source to find the freelancer you need is job boards. Posting on job boards is an easy, proactive way to find freelancers. Although job boards such as Indeed, Glassdoor, and Flexjobs usually charge a small fee or require a subscription in order to list your offer, they typically bring in about 250 applications. However, the downside is that it can take hours to manually go through all of the received applications, especially since not all of these platforms pre-screen applications before they are delivered to you.

Another good option is freelance platforms such as UpWork, Fiverr, Freelancer, Guru, etc. On such platforms, you will have access to a broad pool of talents in different domains. However, there are other platforms solely dedicated to freelancers in specific fields such as 99Designs which is devoted to freelance designers.

Once you receive responses for your job offer, it's time to vet applications. Just as you would vet or interview full-time candidates, you should do the same with freelancers. Typically, you can check a freelancer's rating and reviews by their former clients, as well as samples of their work. All of these details can be incredibly valuable and decisive for your selection criteria and process.

A conference call can be an option at first when you want to get an overall understanding of the freelancer's personality and experience as well as their ability to properly achieve the proposed job as per the given requirements and timeline. Since freelancers typically work with companies for a brief period, it's recommended not to invest a lot of your time and effort in the interview phase. When hiring a freelancer, your goal should be to spend fewer resources while obtaining more results.

I highly recommend that you run a "test task" or a "trial task" where you pick a small section of the project/task you're intending to appoint to a freelancer and just post it online. You can assign it to more than one potential candidate, and then review how they performed that partial task to determine which freelancer best meets your quality expectations.

Once you've selected your ideal freelancer, create a legally binding document that holds both you and the freelancer accountable for the preset terms, deliverables, and compensation. You can use a Statement Of Work, a contract, and even a Non-Disclosure Agreement (NDA) if your business requires it.

You'll also want to document all of your expectations, as well as whatever you approved to grant from your end. Payment method, compensations, quality guidelines, determining deliverables, project deadline, expected availability, confidentiality policy, and the implications of not meeting the project goals, must all be noted and recorded. But, if you choose to use freelance platforms, most of these details are automatically administered and managed through and by the platform.

Once everything is clear and agreed upon by both sides, it's time to sign the contract so your freelancer will be ready to start working. Once you find some talented people that you enjoy working with, keep in touch with them but don't be afraid to venture out and find someone else to do a similar job for you.

Over the years, you'll build up a network of freelancers that you can depend on. When you get to this point, you've already saved significant time by skipping all of the previous steps. Every time you need someone to do a job for you, there will be a database of talents you worked with to choose from. Moreover, you will have freelancers that you trust and thus you can recommend to others. Over time, you may realize that you need full-time staff members, and then you can ask them to work with you instead of freelancing.

***

Here you go, now you know how hiring a great freelancer works. As you can see, hiring a freelancer is actually very similar to hiring a full-time employee. However, as with most things in life, the more times you do it, the easier it gets.

How to document your project?

Short Answer

A solid project documentation process promotes a more organized and systematic tracking of your project progress. You want to start by defining which documents you're going to use throughout the different project phases and processes, then you should create the documents using the suitable tool to write each one of them. Next, you should maintain and update documents throughout the project duration before finally saving and archiving them all for future reference.

Explanation

In order to produce all documents required to successfully execute your project, you need to implement a streamlined, efficient, and standard documentation process. Establishing such a process will provide transparency of your entire workflow as well as visibility throughout every phase of your project.

You should always involve the concerned stakeholders in the process to guarantee their buy-in; it's useless to spend a lot of time creating a document that your client might not approve or even need. On the other hand, leaving out certain documents in other cases is considered a shortfall in the project requirements.

Implementing documents should also follow some rules to ensure a consistent format and compelling content. As a project manager, you should deploy your coaching skills to guide your team on how to create the right documents, the right way, and how to share them with stakeholders at the right time using the right medium.

In this section, we're explaining which documents you will likely need for your project, and how to create, implement, manage, update, and save these required documents.

1. Determining needed documents

Now, we're getting into details, explaining which documents will need to be created in each phase of your project. These documents will cover a wide range of topics, ensuring a steady progression of the project at each step.

The project creation phase takes place at an organizational level since it addresses a company-wide need. This often starts with the project business case document. In this phase, the project's proposition is put forward, outlined, and approved in order to receive the required funding.

Next, the project charter is established to authorize the project initiation. This is an important document in project management as it comprises an outlined description of the project deliverables as well as the major roles and responsibilities of the individuals involved in it.

With the initiation phase being completed, we can now proceed with project planning. During this phase, the project manager develops a thorough plan covering the scope, budget, schedule, risks, acceptance criteria, etc. If the project is relatively small, all of these elements can be gathered in a single document called the "Statement of Work (SOW)".

Followed by the planning activity is the project execution. Now, we're really getting into the thick of it. In this stage, recording events and progress is quite important to make sure that the project work is being implemented according to plan.

Once the project has been completed, and before any celebrations start, you need to formally round things off by carrying out the closure phase. This involves developing a lessons learned register to note what you have learned from the project, as a team. This is an important part of the documentation process as it presents an approach to continuous growth and success in future projects.

Now that you know what documents you need for each project phase, here's how you can actually create these documents.

2. Creating documents

Some online sources, such as ProjectManagementDocs.com, provide free templates for all of the essential project documents that you'll need to create. These prove to be helpful for getting your new project's documentation process up and running as quickly and smoothly as possible. Ready-to-use templates can have different formats like Word, Excel, Google docs or sheets, PowerPoint, etc. So, just choose the best document type according to your needs.

The most important characteristic of good project documentation is consistency. Yes, it is nice and even highly desirable for documents to have a consistent look and feel. But, what matters here is the way consistency can speed up people's ability to find information because they know and recognize a format. Keep in mind that we write documents to communicate with other people. So, never underestimate the value of clear writing.

When it comes to documents' writing and editing, my top advice would be to make your documents:
- **Compelling to read:** by creating a simple structure and offering your readers frequent signposts, so they can easily follow your logic.
- **Easy to read:** by using direct language, with neat formatting and plenty of white space. Try to make your documents as easy to understand as possible, by supplementing your text with illustrations, diagrams, graphs, and tables.
- **Persuasive:** by separating facts from opinion, and recognizing the need to establish trust and credibility.
- **Memorable:** by consistently emphasizing key messages, in different ways.
- **Powerful:** by giving your documents the power to drive actions through setting out clearly, the decisions or actions you need your reader to take.

Presentation is also important. A good starting place is your corporate style guide if you have one. If you don't, look for the best and clearest internal documents, and adapt the used style.

The front page or cover sheet of each document should always include the project name, the Project Manager and Sponsor names, document name, version and date, and document author.
Establishing a uniform set of templates for your team to use is a good practice to ensure that they get their documentation right every time.

3. Implementing documents
Project Managers sometimes "talk the talk" by producing all the necessary documents for their projects. But then they forget them, and do the project on

'gut instinct'. Or, to put it more precisely, they make them up, again, as they go along. Not only is this a serious threat to good governance, but it also undermines your team and stakeholders' confidence in what is going on. Worse than that, creating documents without implementing any is just a plain waste of time and effort.

Security is another important aspect when managing your project documentation. Some companies opt for professional document management tools, such as SharePoint. Whatever option you go for, you should ensure that your documents are secure by taking care of confidentiality, data protection, and unauthorized edits.

4. Maintaining and updating documents

Your documents should be maintained and updated throughout the duration of the project. When you and your team decide on a major change in the project, make sure that all related documentation is updated accordingly.

It's important that people know they are working on the right documents. If a member of the project team updates a document, without telling others, disasters can arise. Two people can be working from different versions of the same document, thus implementing different and inconsistent work. This will result in inefficiency and wasted effort.

You can opt for a version control discipline that ensures three things:
1. There is a central register that allows any user to know the status of any document,
2. Each document contains clear information that allows users to know its status,
3. Users must be able to track changes from one version to another, and so, they can quickly understand the differences that a new version introduces.

With Google Docs, for instance, you can automate storage, recording, and version marking for your documents. However, the documents' basic structure should be built into your templates.

5. Saving and archiving documents

Now that you finished the project, you should save and archive your documents so that you can turn to them as a reference when necessary. Appropriate documentation of past projects could be of great help as you can replicate common elements or layouts for your next project.

Your project documentation is valuable. Therefore, you should treat your documents as assets that need to be taken care of. The first consideration when storing documents is that users can find and access them easily when they need to.

When saving or archiving documents, you should avoid dispersed storage. I usually create a folder for each project and under that folder, I create the following five subfolders:

1. **Agreements**: includes all contractual documents and financial reports. You need to closely manage access to these documents since not all of your team should obtain such information.
2. **Customer resources:** includes all documents provided by the customer. For instance, if you are developing accounting software and the customer sends you their financial report, you should save it under this folder. Also, when customers share links to documents on the cloud, such as Google Docs, make sure to always download and save these documents since you might lose access later on.
3. **Planning:** includes project requirements, schedule, stakeholder list, risk analysis, etc.
4. **Execution:** includes all the documents created to satisfy the project needs. Product design, for example, falls under this folder.
5. **Reports and meetings' notes**: includes status reports and meeting notes, usually shared with the client.

***

To conclude, if you aspire to attain an appropriate level of organization for your project, we've shown you just how much you can benefit from establishing a comprehensive project documentation process.

An efficient system of streamlined, traceable, and functional documentation plays a huge part when it comes to managing every aspect of your projects. This will allow you to lead your projects without a hitch, ticking all the boxes, meeting all deadlines, keeping track of your team's performance, and consistently generating optimal outcomes.

Do you need project management software?

Short Answer
A majority of projects opt for management software nowadays, which makes you wonder: Does every project need project management software? Well, if you happen to manage a big project with large, remote, or dispersed teams, and your project is suffering from poor organization, communication problems, or imperfect planning, then you surely need project management software to prevent and solve such issues. But, if your project is small, simple, and fast, with a process that already works, then you don't have to bother with such a tool.

Explanation
Project management software mainly helps project managers with task allocation, time tracking, budgeting, resource planning, team collaboration, and in further other areas. Project management software is often referred to as Task Management Software or Project Portfolio Management. There are many options on the market including Trello, Monday, Smartsheet, Basecamp, Asana, Jira, Zoho projects, etc.

Deciding on whether your organization needs a project management software or not can take a lot of thinking, especially if it's your first time using one. But, there are a few solid indicators that you might actually need to invest in such a tool. So, how do you tell if your project, your company, or your team can benefit from project management software? Let's find out!

1. When you do need a project management software
If you regularly deal with problems resulting from poor organization, or if you've ever made a mistake at work because you misplaced files or forgot a deadline, this is an obvious sign that you need project management software.

Project management software typically involves many features that will help you and your team become more organized. Apart from providing a space for storing all your project's data including schedules, project milestones, and resource reports, such software also gives you a bird's eye view of everything going on in your project. It allows you for instance to know when something requires your attention in a timely manner.

Another issue that can be tackled and solved using project management software is poor communication amongst project stakeholders. If you have problems keeping the lines of communication open with your project team members, clients, partners, or vendors, project management software has tools that make contacting project stakeholders effortless.

Another sign that it's time to use project management software is when you face difficulties with project planning. If you consistently estimate the time it will take to complete a project inaccurately, causing you to have hard-to-meet deadlines, or if you have trouble allocating the proper budget and resources to a project in the planning stage, project management software can be of assistance.

Since project management software functions as a storage for historical data, it allows you to analyze previous projects timelines and budgets to get a vital insight on how much time did the last marketing project take, for instance, or what was the actual budget used for hosting the previous healthcare conference, etc. With past data saved in the project management software, you can put this information to use to generate more accurate project costs estimates and more realistic timelines for your team.

For the modern organization, the success of a project's initiative will be tied to the tools they use. Spreadsheets are still your go-to tool for basic simple project management, but for centralization, collaboration, sharing information, and time management, spreadsheets can prove to be quite limited. Companies need to manage their projects with intuitive tools, that's why online project management software has grown so popular.

Cost-effectiveness is one of the prime reasons why more and more businesses are now opting for online project management systems. SaaS platforms for instance, typically offer a variety of pricing options depending on the features and account size. Typically, the fee includes IT support, server space, and accessibility both on desktop and mobile. Additionally, the software won't become outdated because the services include regular updates.

However, keep in mind that, despite the numerous advantages of project management software, it is not a magical solution to all of your organization or project issues. Investing in project management software does not turn you into a superhuman project manager. It does, however, provide the tools to become one. This type of software will help you get organized, improving both your project planning and communication.

2. When you don't need a project management software

There are certain situations where project management software would become more of a hindrance than a help. Consequently, you may end up wasting the project money or even worse, time.

Some projects are massive and complex, that's why they need an orchestra's worth of people to pull them off over the course of months and even years. Others, on the other hand, are small and quick and can be completed in a couple of weeks or less. This type of project usually gets done so quickly that managing it via a project management tool can make it take longer than it's supposed to. If your business is modeled on these quick one-off projects, then you don't need any project management software to track them.

Project management software is more effective when coordinating multiple contributors. So, freelancers or solo operators, particularly in creative areas such as writing or graphic design, may not need full-featured project management software to organize their work especially if they're undertaking brief projects such as those mentioned above. They can get away with using a spreadsheet document or a task management application with simpler features instead.

Look at it this way: If it ain't broke, don't fix it. If low-tech methods of managing projects are doing the job for you, why even bother with opting for project management software? Don't feel pressured to upgrade to sophisticated project management software if your people already have a good thing going.

***

As always, the key to knowing whether you should buy something or not is to do a proper evaluation of your requirements and see if the thing you're purchasing is going to make any difference. Remember that businesses are always evolving and changing, so it's a good idea to reevaluate your needs at least once or twice a year.

How to track and measure your project progress and status?

Short Answer

Tracking and measuring your project progress is the only way to know if you're effectively executing the project plan. Setting deadlines can be your way to figure out whether or not you're meeting your planned progress. Milestones are also an excellent technique to track progress on a larger scale.

Monitoring the budget and duration forecast can give you an overview of how much is your project meeting its defined goals. This task should not involve only you but the whole team should take part by providing regular status updates and reports. You can also opt for a lot of specialized tools to help you properly perform this task.

Explanation

One of the most substantial parts of a project manager's job is measuring the project's progress and status. Such a step helps project managers keep track of what's happening in their projects, help everyone stay on track, keep team members engaged, and hold all parties accountable.

Tracking your project can allow you to compare the current progress to the forecasted one in order to detect any problems that might prevent the project from remaining on schedule and within budget. The key to project tracking is the creation of status reports that provide an overview of where the project is at any particular time. Other types of project reports can showcase more details to offer a deeper insight into deliverables, progress, and performance. These reports should be shared with the project team and stakeholders in order to keep everyone up to date.

Knowing your actual progress allows you to identify necessary changes, resist possible scope creep, and evaluate likely outcomes at the upcoming stages. For different projects, different metrics are key for evaluating how your project's current status complies with the planned progress level. Mostly, hard numeric values are tracked and assessed such as budgets, schedules, time estimates, worked hours, etc. However, qualitative indicators, such as customer satisfaction or employees' loyalty, matter too.

1. Establishing clear deadlines

Keeping the end goal in sight is always helpful for tracking progress. Setting clear deadlines enables your team to stay on track and accomplish tasks without becoming frustrated or overwhelmed. Once everyone is on the same page about the project timeframe, tracking progress becomes much easier.

Therefore, some project managers tend to work with one final deadline, whilst others prefer to set different deadlines for each milestone or goal. Whatever method you prefer and use, keeping track of your project should be a simple matter of sticking to the schedule as long as every deadline is properly defined and team members have a clear understanding of what they're working towards.

2. Planning milestones

Working with team members to generate your project outline can be a great way for tracking project progress. Each team member can give input for setting up realistic project goals and learning what's expected of them both individually and collectively as a team. A good first step is to sit down with your team to create a comprehensive outline, including milestones and Key Performance Indicators (KPIs).

Setting up tailored goals and milestones for each team member significantly contributes to team satisfaction. However, keeping the big picture in mind is also important, especially when implementing smaller goals and points of progress.

Even small projects should include a number of milestones to mark the completion of major phases, events, or tasks along your project timeline. Some project managers create and maintain a separate document for milestones such as the one we're providing a template for.

3. Time and budget monitoring

Timesheets provide you with a clear way to measure progress as long as you use the data in there appropriately. For example, just because it took someone 16 hours to work on a certain task does not mean that it is close to completion, even if it is supposed to mainly take 20 hours. You'll need to combine tracking data with other information, such as speaking with the team member executing the task to gain a sense of how close they are to completing the work at hand.

One of the advantages of time tracking is that it does give you early oversight if something is going to be delayed. You can typically see from a timesheet that someone is working far more or far fewer hours than you would expect, and that should give you a reason to be concerned.

Likewise, monitoring the project's budget is essential for ensuring profitability. An important part of budget monitoring is staying aware of project costs. You should always keep track of the current costs of your employees' work, and analyze their structure. The obtained data can be used for the calculation of various indicators of project success such as keeping track of project profitability as a ratio of costs against billable amounts. Thus, you should consider setting up a report that automatically calculates this proportion and then run it on major project steps to see the dynamics.

More importantly, don't forget to monitor the balance between forecasted and actual costs. If actual costs exceed the planned ones, try to figure out what are the reasons for the cost increase, and how it is affecting the project profitability. Moreover, calculating earned value will let you see how much value project costs bring. You can use earned value data to identify whether budget adjustments are necessary or not.

The analysis of your project costs structure should also be part of your budget monitoring. It's not uncommon that tasks not billable to clients consume a large part of your employees' work time, thus undermining your project profitability. Identify how non-billable works affect the resulting value of the project, and consider using it as an opportunity to cut project costs.

4. Regular check-ins and status reporting

When considering how to track your project progress, never underestimate the importance of regular check-ins. Having a quick, informal chat at the start of each work session can establish trust between a project manager and his team.

Communication is always key to make sure a project is running smoothly. If a team member is having trouble reaching a pre-set goal or performing time-sensitive tasks, it's better to check in with them and try to figure out the reason behind it, rather than showing dissatisfaction. You can also set regular project status meetings, where your team needs to prepare and submit reports, questionnaires, or any other form of feedback on the project status and progress.

The key point here is collecting actual data on possible issues and difficulties, and being able to take action as soon as possible. During such meetings, you should listen to your team's feedback and encourage them to communicate more. Always remind your team how timely reporting of possible issues is important for the successful delivery of the project.

This part of monitoring is hard to automate, but developing an informative and consistent survey or report form makes data analysis easier and allows you to reveal important trends and risks.

***

In reality, a combination of all these methods is the ideal way to track and measure your project progress. For some tasks, you'll calculate time spent, while for others, you'll size the percentage of work completed. Thus, use your best judgment, select a method that works best for your project, and of course, don't be afraid to mix them up and use multiple approaches at once.

What are the main project management KPIs?

Short Answer
Major project management key performance indicators (KPIs) fall under four categories: Timeliness, Budget, Quality, and Effectiveness. Timeliness KPIs will help you make sure your project is done on time. On the other hand, Budget KPIs will help you track if your project is staying under the budget you've allocated or is exceeding costs. KPIs like Customer complaints or Number of errors fall under the quality category. Finally, you can track and measure Effectiveness through KPIs like the Number of project milestones completed on time.

Explanation
Keeping track of key performance indicators is essential when executing a project. Without KPIs, it's difficult to follow how you're progressing toward your goals. But, how do you know what you should measure for each project? Overwhelming your team with data won't make the project succeed. However, monitoring the right data ensures the project stays on track.

The first step is to decide which project management KPIs to track and measure. Next, you have to define your KPIs in a clear and focused manner. There are many project management KPI templates that you can use to guide you through this process. But, it's important to keep in mind that the chosen KPIs should be S.M.A.R.T; Specific, Measurable, Achievable, Relevant, and Time-Bound. Also, your KPIs should be agreed upon by all involved parties before initiating a project, and then measured and monitored as a tool for decision-making during the project.

SMART Goals

These are the four main categories of project management KPIs that we're going through: Timeliness, Budget, Quality, and Effectiveness.

1. Timeliness

Timeliness KPIs are used to ensure your project is completed on time. If it's not, tracking where it goes off-target is crucial in order to be able to fix any underlying issues and to estimate an accurate completion date.

This category involves the KPIs like:
- **Cycle Time:** This is the time needed to complete a specific task or activity. This is helpful for repeated tasks in a project.
- **On-time Completion Percentage:** to find out how many tasks are completed by their pre-set deadlines.
- **Time Spent**: indicating the amount of time spent on the project by all team members, or by each team member individually. This KPI's measurement could be in hours, calendar days, full-time equivalent work days, weeks, or months.
- **Schedule Variance (SV) & Schedule Performance Index (SPI)**: measure schedule performance based on the Earned Value (which refers to the value of the work accomplished to date) and the Planned Value (PV). Their equations are as follows:
  $SV = EV - PV$ and $SPI = EV / PV$.

2. Budget

Budget KPIs will enable you to figure out if your project is going to stay under the budget you've allocated, or if it is going to exceed costs.

This KPIs category mainly involves:
- **Actual Cost (AC):** is the amount of money that you have spent on an ongoing project so far.
- **Planned Value (PV):** is the authorized planned budget for accomplishing the work of an activity or a project. For example, if we have a 2-month project with a $10,000 budget, after one month the PV will be $5,000.
- **Earned Value (EV):** is the value that the project has produced to date. For example, let's assume we have a $30,000 project that should be completed in 3 months. After 2 months you spent $25,000 and achieved

only 50% of the work. The EV is $15,000. NB: In this case, the PV = $20,000 and the AC = $25,000.

- **Cost Variance (CV) & Cost Performance Index (CPI):** measure cost performance by comparing the budgeted cost of the work you've completed so far (EV) to the actual amount spent (AC). Referring to the above example: CV = EV - AC = -$10,000 and CPI = EV / AC = 0.6, which indicates that the project is over budget.

3. Quality

How well has the project progressed? Are those working on it or benefitting from it satisfied?

To answer these questions, you'll have to rely on Quality KPIs such as:

- **Customer Satisfaction or Loyalty:** to figure out whether or not someone is satisfied and would work with you again. A survey is an efficient way to figure that out.
- **Number Of Errors:** represents the number of times your team had to redo or rework something, which directly affects your project's budget and schedule revisions.
- **Customer Complaints:** Counts how many times your customer complained due to not getting what they are expecting.
- **Employee Churn Rate:** The percentage or number of team members who have left the company. If your project team has a high turnover rate, it may be a sign that your management and work environment needs urgent improvement. Churn ultimately slows down projects and creates higher costs for the company in the long run. Let's say you started the project with 20 team members and after one year you lose 5 of them, then your churn rate is (5 / 20) x 100 = 25%.

4. Effectiveness

Finally, in this category, we'll identify some KPIs that will help you figure out if you're spending your time and money efficiently and appropriately or not.

Effectiveness KPIs include:

- **Number of Milestones Completed On Time:** to measure whether each of the project phases is being completed in a timely manner. A milestone is considered achieved when it's approved and signed off by all involved parties.

- **Number of Returns:** If your project requires delivering many items, you may want to track the return rate of those items; this helps you assess if you did a good job planning or adapting to the project requirements during implementation.
- **Number of Change Requests:** is the number and frequency at which a client requests changes to an agreed-upon scope of work. Too many alterations can negatively affect the project budget, resources, timeline, and overall quality.
- **Billable Utilization:** The percentage of project hours you can actually charge a client for. Billable hours relate to profit-generating and project-related tasks, while unbillable hours typically involve administrative tasks, such as drafting and negotiating proposals.

***

A project has many moving parts, and it is critical that you measure its timeliness, budget, quality, and effectiveness along the way in order to ensure you are executing your project effectively, within budget, and within deadlines.

When trying to choose and short-list KPIs, make sure to start with a business context. A good strategy map, for instance, would be really helpful. Also, try to define your KPIs properly, understand the distinction between leading and lagging indicators and the difference between success factors and success criteria, and most importantly, keep your list short. A pair of leading and lagging indicators for each goal will work much better than a list of dozens of metrics.

How to measure your team's motivation?

Short Answer

The two main metrics that can help you measure your team's motivation are performance metrics and satisfaction Indicators. Of course, measuring both individual and team satisfaction is merely the first step; what really matters is how to improve your team's wellbeing and prosperity. Refer to the third section of this book addressing "Communication" to find the practical details on how to motivate your team.

Explanation

Good teamwork is the basis of any successful project. The key to effective teamwork, however, is the full engagement of the project manager. High engagement promotes values such as teamwork, collaboration, devotion, etc. in order to ensure efficient performance. In order to assess your team's satisfaction and performance, you should monitor, track, and measure your contributors' work execution. But, which metrics should you keep an eye on?

1. Performance metrics

The essence of a team's performance is collaborating and being present to support each other. While this can be a hard metric to track, it is essential for improving productivity. Your team's performance table should include the presence metric as you should keep track of it daily.

Presence has different dimensions. I once worked remotely for a company where you'll only be considered present when you are active on Slack or when you promptly respond to messages.

On the other hand, commitment and productivity go hand in hand. Thus, if you aspire to increase your team's productivity on a certain project, you must keep track of their commitment. The best way to do that is to track how much time they're spending on project activities and focus on the quality of their outputs.

Missing deadlines and poor deliverables are major indicators of a lack of commitment. I once managed an engineer with high performance. However, during the project, his productivity dropped drastically. The first indicator was his recurrent standup meeting absence. Then, his work performance started to suffer; he had a low working pace and made many errors revealing his lack of attention.

Someone can spend hours and hours working on their tasks, but if their work lacks quality it won't improve the project's productivity or profitability. In order to track the work quality metric, you need to have some knowledge of each of your team member's assignments.

By talking with them about their progress and checking on their work, you will be able to see whether they have to improve their work quality or if it is satisfactory. This doesn't mean that you should stand over their heads and watch over their every move. All you have to do is to spare some time for checking what they are doing and more importantly how they are doing it.

2. Satisfaction index

To determine your team members' satisfaction rate, you should create a survey and ask them to fill it out. The survey should assess the following: pay satisfaction, growth prospects, job stress levels, benefits, workload, overall climate, the extent to which executives practice organizational values, supervisor competence, the openness of communication, physical environment or ergonomics, and trust.

Then, you may need to find out the following rates to obtain a more accurate insight into your team satisfaction: voluntary turnover rate, rate of complaints or grievances, absenteeism rate, rate of transfer requests, etc.

You can also opt for focus groups to gather more in-depth qualitative information on the survey items or address any revealed issues that your team is facing. However, for individual concerns, you should set up a one-on-one meeting and try to openly discuss what didn't work and what should be improved.

***

Your project will always depend on how your team members perform their tasks. Even the best leaders can't succeed on their own, as they need a good team to execute and achieve the project vision. The key to an accomplishing team is measuring its performance and constantly motivating them to further improve their efficiency. Measuring the team's performance through the presented metrics will help you spot the weak points and handle them accordingly.

How to deliver a project without issues or bugs?

Short Answer

Delivering a project with no issues or bugs might sound hard to achieve, but by allowing adequate time for testing, evaluation, and defect correction in your estimates you can identify and work on any issues before delivering the product. Timing is key upon issues identification, as they should be reported promptly.

Also, you should have a system for collecting issues and tracking the progress of their resolution. As the Project Manager, you should foster the creation of similar processes not only to prevent issues or bugs from happening in the first place but also to handle them effectively once they occur.

Explanation

The stepping stone to successful projects is appropriate planning. Planning includes but is not limited to the project's schedule, budget, scope, risks, resources, quality, etc. However, some project managers fail to understand the importance of quality planning; they either postpone or neglect inspections or improvements claiming that their teams are already overwhelmed with project activities. This will eventually force them to put everything on hold in order to fix occurring issues and bugs, and even then, it might be too late to save the whole project from failure.

But, even when you thoroughly plan your project, taking all the required measures to ensure quality, issues can still arise. Thus, if you want your project to succeed, you must have a plan in place to quickly and effectively respond to any issues once they happen. These next steps are part of the best practices to implement in order to make sure you'll deliver your product with fewer issues or bugs.

1. Planning for testing

As your plans and final requirement definitions come together, you should include well-defined activities for gaining final approval. Start by identifying the contributors who will own the testing and evaluation tasks at project closure, and work with them to define, estimate, and schedule them.

First, you should review all performance and acceptance criteria with your customer, and adjust your plans accordingly whenever you agree to any updates or changes. You must always allow adequate time for testing, evaluation, and defect correction in your estimates.

You should also refer to similar recently executed projects during the planning phase. If the retrospective analysis of previous projects shows systemic closure issues, you should review their root causes to avoid repeating the same mistakes.

Whether you adopt a step-by-step approach to your work or not, plan for periodic check-ins with your users, customers, and stakeholders during your project. Include scheduled reviews of proofs-of-concept, prototypes, pilots, or other interim deliverables, and encourage participation by people who will be responsible for final approval in inspections, component tests, and other early evaluations. The feedback from these activities can provide you with an early warning system for potential and more serious problems that can occur later on.

2. Implementing a system

Without a process or a tool to report the detected issue, the latter will be lost in the shuffle of the project. Thus, you need a way to report on issues collaboratively, so that every team member will be notified and aware of the present and past issues and their status.

For small projects, creating an online collaborative document should be enough to collect and track issues' progress. This is commonly known as an "issue log" or "issue tracking". It is used to identify, describe, prioritize, and assign an owner for each detected issue.

ID	Description	Reported by	Reported date	Assigned to	Priority	Status	Resolution/ Comments
001	Scraping script is not working	Monica	13/07/2021	Sergio	High	Closed	The problem is caused by the last version update. Resolved on 14/07/2021.
002	Search functionality is taking too long	Markus	20/07/2021	Markus	Low	Open	
003	Search error when entering more than 100 characters	Markus	25/07/2021	Sergio	Medium	Open	

Issue log sample

However, a system is usually better for tracking issues. Your project management software can work for tracking issues. A separate ticketing application can do the job too. Such a system will provide you with more flexibility, allowing you to link issues, get statistics, archive old issues, etc.

3. Managing issues and bugs

When dealing with bugs and issues, timing is key. If you allow reporting to lag, you lose the opportunity to resolve the issue before it becomes too large to fix or requires so many resources as to be a project-buster. Communication is important and channels must be open to get that information out to the right people as fast as possible. If you're reporting promptly, you should resolve the issue appropriately and quickly.

Upon identifying an issue, start by assigning a team member to handle it. If you put more than one person in charge, ensure that only one is accountable. Issues are only resolved when there is clear ownership. If resolving the identified issue is not moving smoothly, try to figure out why. It could be that the assessment wasn't accurate or that there are secondary risks that the team member is trying to tackle instead. When detected problems are being fixed, you should watch out for any resulting scope creep as the planned work might exceed or change the initial scope.

***

Issues are unavoidable. They're a part of managing any project. Setting up an effective issues management process will give you a robust way of identifying and documenting issues and problems that occur during a project. Such a process will also make it easier to evaluate these issues, assess their impact, and decide on a resolution plan. An issue log allows you to capture the details of every issue so that the project team can be continuously aware of its current status and especially who's responsible for resolving it.

When you set up an issue management framework, you have a thorough plan to handle the detected issues quickly and efficiently. This methodical approach to managing and solving issues and bugs results in valuable insights that can be utilized to refine and improve future project results.

Moreover, effective collaboration is essential for identifying, prioritizing, and treating bugs. An agile team that coherently works together in real-time will be able to recognize defects in their products and mitigate them more quickly. This also shortens development and testing cycles, boosts team efficiency, and reduces the time needed to deliver high-quality software to market.

How to wrap up a project?

Short Answer

There's a lot of work involved even when a project is technically complete. The first step to wrapping up a project is completing paperwork. Projects generate a number of documents that must get signed off, approved by stakeholders, and archived. Next, you should gather the core team to invite feedback about what did and didn't work, and discuss learnings and reviews. You may also want to celebrate the project's success with the involved parties so it would be the final step before moving forward.

Explanation

The closure phase is the final step in a project's life cycle, marking your project's official completion. When the project closure phase is accomplished properly, your project documents should be finalized, your clients and stakeholders should have any final reports that they require, and your team should have had the chance to reflect upon and adjust their processes.

A project closure procedure must take place so that you can cover every base and move on to your next mission. The following are the main steps you should take to make sure you've dotted all the I's and crossed all the T's, as well as ensuring you've taken full advantage of the whole experience.

1. Paperwork and formalities

At the end of the project, some documents have to get signed off and approved by all of the involved stakeholders. This needs a lot of attention, as these documents are the legal proof that, in fact, you have concluded the project. This also includes closing all contracts you might have made with internal partners or vendors or any other resources you worked with. Don't forget to treat all outstanding payments. You want to make sure that all invoices, commissions, fees, bonuses, etc. are paid.

Along with technical updates of documents, contracts, and payment, make sure the project is closed properly from an administrative perspective. Check that everyone has put their files on the server and that those folders and files are archived and stored in a well-ordered manner. You should set a clear organizational pattern established long before the project gets started.

Make sure all final versions are appropriately labeled before archiving any documents. You should be doing this from the project start, but now, during project closure, it's time to dive in and make sure everything is as it should be. Don't forget to go through your issues log to make sure all were dealt with, and check your risks report to make sure there are no unresolved risks.

Finally, since you learned so much over the course of your project lifecycle, you sure don't want any valuable information to be forgotten or go to waste just because the project is finished. So, after dealing with collecting project phases records, you should take care of managing the transfer of knowledge, and identifying lessons learned.

2. Learnings, feedback, and reviews

There are always lessons to be learned from projects, that is why you meet with your team regularly to look back on your processes. But, if you don't have an archive from which you retrieve old data or records, then whatever knowledge you acquired will be lost and forgotten.

For feedback, write a note to your team mentioning something specific to each team member. Sure, you can copy-paste a generic "Yay! we've made it" email and hit send. But, your team is going to feel that it's inauthentic, and they're right. Instead, focus on something each team member did really well and commend them for it. Make your closure email specific and thoughtful.

Did you notice any errors, missing items, or needed follow-ups during your project clean-up? Take your time to write these into the closure email too and explain the "next steps" for how each is going to be addressed.

Don't forget about your client. Asking for feedback should be a constant element of your process, but there are different ways to go about this. In some cases, simply asking a few casual questions in an email is more than enough. But, ideally, getting testimonials and asking for permission to share them on the company's website and on social media channels would be even better.

Even if your project was uncomplicated and went smoothly, a retrospective meeting should take place before closure, as it is not only meant to showcase how to fix things that went wrong, it's also meant to show what went right, and how to replicate that over other projects.

You should also consider presenting an anonymous survey to your team. An anonymous survey is an excellent approach to elicit candid feedback from people who are uncomfortable with confrontation. Use straightforward simple questions with multiple-choice answers for the best results. You should also leave room for free flow notes and comments.

You don't want to put much time into a retrospective feedback meeting and then just toss it out or forget the results. All of the collected information is going to make you a better project team in the future. That's why we recommend putting together a final report of lessons learned, making sure your team has taken part in identifying them and that they read the report thoroughly.

3. Celebrating and moving forward

Celebrating is a form of reward and acknowledgment to your team that they have done a great job. When you note a job well done you boost morale, making your team members feel appreciated. This creates loyalty, thus they will work even harder on the next project. Plus, there surely will be another common endeavor, because a happy team is one that sticks around.

After celebrating your success, you should think about your next step. Create a roadmap for moving forward based on what you have learned. A roadmap can allow you to carefully define your next opportunity and work on it.

Don't forget to update your credentials. Have your professional records reflect this most recent completed achievement. As you're going to be searching for a new challenge, pitching yourself for your next project requires updating your resume. Moreover, it's way easier to update your resume at the end of the closure phase of your project when all the details are still firm in your mind.

Alongside your personal profiles, your company probably has its own set of sources and websites that you will want to update with this most recently completed project. For example, you may want to update your organization's portfolio on their website or on their presentation decks.

***

It's so tempting to just move to the next thing after a project finishes. The extra time and energy to do even more work seem daunting, but it's really in your best interest as a project manager to close a project properly.

V. Agile

Nowadays, the Agile approach is increasingly adopted. With time, more projects are transitioning from Waterfall to the Agile model especially in the IT field. However, despite its popularity and multiple benefits, the Agile approach has several challenges that work behind its failover.

According to the Project Management Institute (PMI), the challenges of Agile are associated with an inadequate experience with agile methods, little understanding of the required broader organizational change, or company philosophy or culture at odds with agile values.

In this section of the book, we are going to discover the principles of Agile and the practices of one of its most prevalent frameworks, i.e., Scrum. We are going to address the common misconceptions and inquiries concerning Agile in order to provide you with a more clear understanding of this approach.

What is the difference between Agile and Scrum?

Short answer

The primary distinction between Agile and Scrum is that Agile is a project management philosophy based on a core set of principles or values, whereas Scrum is a specific Agile framework used to facilitate a project. While Agile involves members from diverse cross-functional teams, a Scrum project team implies specific roles, like the Scrum Master and Product Owner. It's important to understand that even though Scrum is an Agile approach, Agile does not always mean Scrum; there are many other frameworks that take an Agile approach for running a project.

Explanation

A project life cycle is made up of a series of phases that every project goes through from its start to its completion. A project can follow a predictive or adaptive life cycle. The latter can be either iterative, incremental, or both. This approach is also known as agile or change-driven where change has a high probability, and the project team works closely with project stakeholders.

Scrum is an agile framework that combines iterative and incremental development life cycles. It's so common that people often confuse it with Agile. Given their similarities, it's easy to understand why they can sometimes be easily confused, but they are actually two distinct concepts. Here's a breakdown of how these two terms differ from one another:

1. Agile

The literal meaning of the word Agile is "being able to move quickly and easily". In project management, Agile is a set of principles that is particularly popular in the IT industry. Agile Software Development Manifesto was established in 2001 defining the Agile values as follows: Individuals and interactions over processes and tools, working software over comprehensive documentation, customer collaboration over contract negotiation, and responding to change over following a plan.

Agile is best understood in terms of how it differs from the traditional method of project management, i.e., waterfall, serial, plan-driven, or predictive. The latter is characterized by a linear sequential approach that usually involves: initiation, planning, execution, monitoring, and closing. However, the Agile project management approach is rather characterized by a non-linear approach. Instead of being set and defined in the planning phase, requirements evolve and emerge throughout the project duration.

Triangle of Constraints: Agile vs. Waterfall

The Agile method is increasingly popular due to its focus on teamwork and collaboration among self-organizing, cross-functional teams. Besides, it generates constant value through the combination of iterative and incremental life cycles.

There are many different approaches used to implement the Agile philosophy. Some of the most common involve Scrum, Kanban, Feature Driven Development (FDD), Extreme Programming (XP), Lean Software Development (LSD), Adaptive System Development (ASD), Dynamic Systems Development Method (DSDM), and Crystal Clear.

2. Scrum

The main fundamental difference between Scrum and Agile is the fact that Scrum represents one of the numerous approaches for implementing Agile. Scrum is one of the most opted for Agile frameworks. It relies on an iterative and incremental approach in which incremental builds are delivered to the customer every one to four weeks. These cycles are commonly known as Sprints.

Throughout the Sprint, the development team holds a daily stand-up meeting to ensure that everyone is on the same page and that they have an encompassing insight into what is going on, whether it's good or bad. Usually, such a meeting takes up to 15 minutes where every team member is asked three questions: What did you do yesterday that helped your team meet the Sprint Goal? What will you do today to help your team meet the Sprint goal? And, Did you face any impediments that prevented you or your team from meeting the Sprint goal?

At the end of each sprint, the development team demonstrates the completed features in front of the Product Owner (PO) and key stakeholders in order to receive feedback. This product-centric meeting is known as Sprint Review.

When it comes to process improvement, the Sprint Retrospective meeting is dedicated to discussing what went well and what measures should be undertaken to increase work efficiency and quality. This meeting takes place after the Sprint Review and before the following Sprint Planning. The retrospective meeting is considered as a meeting for improvement, as it is mainly held to find the proper ways and means of identifying potential pitfalls and past errors, and to seek out new ways to avoid those mistakes.

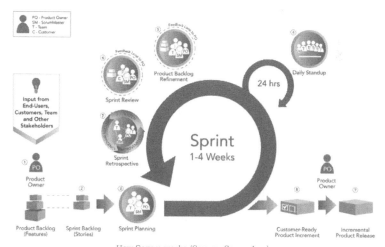

How Scrum works (Source: Scrum Inc.)

***

Upon understanding the difference between these two terms, a project team should determine whether it would be advantageous to use an Agile approach for their project. They should decide what will bring better results; Scrum or another Agile framework. This choice mainly depends on the project type as well as the company's culture.

Is the Agile approach right for your project?

Short Answer

Nowadays, Agile seems to be a no-brainer choice for software projects due to these projects' high frequency of requirements updates and technological changes. However, if your project exists in a heavily regulated industry where you have to provide extensive documentation and exhaustive planning, an agile approach might not be convenient for your project since Agile emphasizes responding to change over following a plan.

Explanation

One of the first choices you'll have to make with each project implementation is "Which life cycle should we opt for?" Taking this decision often leads to heated debates and generates a lot of discussions.

In this section, we're explaining how choosing a life cycle depends on the project and the enterprise environmental factors, and how you can assess these key factors to eventually decide which approach between Agile and Waterfall is more suitable for your project.

1. When is Agile suitable for your project?

Agile relies on a high level of customer involvement throughout the project's lifecycle, as the customer has early and frequent opportunities to see the work being delivered, as well as make decisions and changes throughout the development phase. The customer also gains a strong sense of ownership by working extensively and directly with the project team throughout the project.

If time to market a certain application is of greater concern than releasing a complete feature set at the initial launch, Agile can quickly produce a basic version of working software that can be improved in the successive iterations (aka functional or shippable product increments).

Another aspect of Agile is that it works best for small teams of 3 to 9 people. If you cannot execute your project through small teams or groups for whatever reason, then Agile is not right for you.

The greatest advantage of the agile approach is its flexibility. If there are any issues or changes, they can easily and rapidly adjust product requirements and goals. However, if the customer is not involved enough, then Agile will not give you the results you are aspiring for.

You should also consider the technology involved in the project. The agile approach, being more flexible, allows for more experimentation with new technologies. Whereas the traditional project management methodology is more appropriate if no new technology or tools are involved.

Is your project highly prone to risks and threats? Given the rigid nature of traditional approaches, it's not recommended to use them in this case. However, since risks can be addressed sooner in the agile approach, it makes it a better option in terms of risk management.

2. When is a traditional approach suitable for your project?

Projects with predetermined outcomes and timescales typically work best using traditional project methodologies. Likewise, projects that need to deliver against very specific, often legal or regulatory requirements, aren't agile-appropriate either. In such projects, requirements and delivery timeframes are very explicit, often with penalties charged when failing to meet them.

For instance, a data center migration project is less likely to be managed through an agile approach, due to the specific requirements concerning networking, heating, ventilation, air-conditioning, hardware, and so on.

In some cases, even if the project happens to be suitable for agile, it might be that the organization is simply not ready yet to make the required cultural transition. A company that is attached to the traditional project mindset will find it hard to shift successfully to agile. Therefore, a hybrid approach could be deployed to ease the transition.

For proper implementation of the Agile approach, teams must be cross-functional as well as being prepared to work within an environment where they are granted the autonomy they need to succeed. The project manager, on the other hand, should play more the role of a facilitator by removing impediments and serving the team. If none of these shifts in roles occur, then agile isn't the route to take.

***

In reality, there is no "all-purpose" or "one size fits all" approach that is suitable for every project or organization. The decision to use a certain approach largely depends on the project's nature, size, available resources, and many other factors. When deciding to opt for an Agile framework for your project, you should consider adapting its practices according to your specific needs. Keep in mind that Agile is not the goal, it's just an instrument to pave your project's success.

How is a Scrum team structured?

Short Answer

A typical Scrum team involves 3 main roles: Scrum Master, Product Owner, and Development Team. The Scrum Master is the one accountable for the proper implementation of the Scrum framework, making sure the Development team is quite efficient through blocking any interruptions and distractions that may affect their performance. The Product Owner, being the voice of the client, is responsible for ensuring that requirements are being met through prioritizing the work to be done. The Development Team in Scrum should be autonomous and self-organized, cross-functional, and collectively accountable for the implemented work.

A Scrum team, including Scrum Master and Product Owner, should never involve more than 9 people. For large projects, team members could be grouped in smaller Scrum teams that collaborate and coordinate work together, aka the Scrum of Scrum technique.

Explanation

Scrum is one of the Agile frameworks. The term "Scrum" is derived from a rugby term that refers to teammates interlocking their arms to push forward into opponents. In the project management field, Scrum is an approach that consists of highly coordinated teamwork, strong organization, and delivering projects according to client requirements.

Unlike traditional development teams, Scrum teams do not have a structural hierarchy. Instead, they are cross-functional and self-managing. Each team member is equally valuable and they all have the necessary skills and expertise for delivering a working product.

Scrum specifies three major roles within a Scrum Team, i.e., Product Owner, Scrum Master, and Development team, all of which we're going to examine in detail.

1. Scrum Master

The term "master" when referring to this role isn't used to indicate someone who has others working for them. It's used in the sense of "a specialist of a particular subject" as this role requires a very strong grasp of the Scrum framework compared to others involved in the project.

The Scrum Master's responsibility involves supervising and coaching the Scrum team. Therefore, they must be aware of all of the Agile values and Scrum practices. Some companies opt for external agile coaches when this role is vacant or the assigned Scrum Master does not have the required experience yet.

Another important responsibility of the Scrum Master is to protect the development team and make sure that everyone can focus on their work with minimal distractions. This includes isolating and handling impediments that come up. They're also responsible for protecting the Scrum process itself by ensuring it's properly applied.

The Scrum Master should follow a servant leadership style. The Agile Practice Guide describes a servant leader as one who promotes self-awareness, listens to their team and serves them, assists people in their development and growth, coaches rather than controls, and promotes security, respect, and trust. Servant leaders prioritize the needs of others, helping them reach their best performance and potential.

2. Product Owner

The word "owner" here refers to responsibility. The Product Owner owns the responsibility of ensuring that the product will be accurately developed. In Scrum, the person in this position represents the customer and works to ensure that their vision is fulfilled.

The Product Owner should be always available to respond to the project team inquiries. They can be considered as the project compass, but that doesn't mean they're the ones running the team or instructing them on how to undertake work.

The product owner is in charge of laying out and prioritizing the work that has to be done. They are knowledgeable in the project expectations and they act as a guide to the team carrying out the project. Product Owners are involved in the project throughout its entire lifespan. They make sure that the product is adjusted and evolving as required in response to market and end-user feedback.

Practically, the Product Owner is responsible for maintaining and refining the product backlog. Leading backlog refinement or grooming sessions with the development team throughout the sprints is required in order to discuss requirements and make user stories and tasks ready for execution in the upcoming sprints.

3. Development team

The development team involves the individuals in charge of writing the code or implementing the project work. The development team can include architects, testers, developers, designers, etc. The team works together, based on the priority set up by the Product Owner, to reach the objectives of each sprint.

Development Teams are self-organizing as no one, not even the Scrum Master, tells them how to turn product backlog into increments of potentially releasable functionality. They are cross-functional as they have all of the required skills to create a product Increment.

Scrum doesn't define any titles for the Development Team members, regardless of the work being performed by the person; testing, architecture, DevOps, security analysis, etc. Even when team members have specialized skills and areas of focus, accountability still belongs to the entire Development Team.

Scrum teams are also designed to anticipate and adapt to change. Scrum, along with other Agile frameworks, makes it easy for teams to pivot based on user feedback and all changing requirements. Consequently, agile teams are more able to deliver higher quality products with greater consistency.

Transparency and communication are key principles of the Scrum framework. The Product Owner and stakeholders are actively involved in the development process to ensure the work is always in line with the product goals and requirements. With higher-quality deliverables, responsive feedback cycles, clear communication, and well-defined scopes, it is no wonder that Scrum teams often achieve higher user satisfaction.

Scrum fosters a collaborative culture with developers being at the heart of the Scrum team. Because there isn't a traditional hierarchy with a team boss, and the work itself is collectively undertaken, team members have a shared sense of ownership for the product. This sense of ownership boosts morale, gives the team a purpose, and improves everyone's work productivity.

***

When forming a Scrum team from scratch, you should have a clear understanding of the purpose and roles, as clarity will certainly help you form an effective team. A Scrum Team is structured to fulfill one common goal: working together to develop the best product capable of satisfying users' expectations. For a Scrum team to constantly deliver value, all three main roles must commit to the process and collaborate to ensure collective growth.

How to define and prioritize tasks on the product backlog?

Short Answer

The Backlog transforms a product's high-level vision into manageable and executable tasks. Before creating the product backlog items, you should define the high-level scope of the project and its success criteria. Once set up, and with the help of the development team, the Product Owner should lead the creation and the prioritization of the backlog.

Explanation

We generally opt for prioritization because we have limited time for every set of items to execute. That's why you have to start with the most important functionalities first.

Projects are apt to be more successful when clients get valued functionalities as early as possible, and that's only achievable by effectively and consistently prioritizing requirements or user stories.

Prioritizing product backlog items is influenced by many factors including customer satisfaction, business value, complexity, risk and opportunity, and cost. However, how does the prioritization process actually take place? That's what we're explaining below.

1. Defining releases or milestones

The goal of initial release planning is to roughly estimate which features will be delivered by the release deadline, presuming the deadline is fixed, or to choose a rough delivery date for a given set of features if the scope is fixed.

To successfully define your releases, you'll need to start by defining your product vision. The vision will guide subsequent decisions concerning which features should be prioritized, where to focus resources and effort, and how to adapt if the project requires adjustment during development.

Next, you will need to review your product backlog and rank the features. Use the product vision as well as inputs from stakeholders to determine product priorities and map out user stories. During this step, the product manager should outline a basic release plan or roadmap that includes the release goal, release target date, and the sorted user stories.

Once the overall product vision and release map are outlined, a release planning meeting should be scheduled to review the proposed plan and modify it as required. At this stage, you should decide on the "Definition of Done" for the given release and review the acceptance criteria for all its user stories.

Following the planning meeting, you should share the product release calendar with all stakeholders. Everyone should have access to the release plan for reference and updates.

Milestones, on the other hand, are an excellent tool for illustrating your project plan progress. They help motivate and align your team by allowing everyone to view their work progress and assess priorities. Milestones can also help you keep an eye on deadlines, identify significant dates, and recognize potential roadblocks within the project.

There is no standard number of milestones every project should have. Some projects will only have two to three milestones, while others may have as many as a dozen. So, rather than attempting to reach a certain number of milestones, you should only set milestones for significant events that are planned to occur during the course of your project.

2. Building the product backlog

Your backlog should be structured, organized, and arranged to prioritize the most strategically important tasks for your team to execute.

The Product Owner is the one in charge of feeding the backlog. Their first step should involve identifying sources that can suggest potential features for the backlog. These sources include user experience or interface research (UI/UX), a specific customer request, a survey, or detailed marketing research.

As they use the product extensively, end-users can be excellent sources for backlog items by providing valuable feedback for improvements. Also, your customer support feedback is a decent source as it can report problems or issues from the field. Feedback and reviews concerning the product's problems, issues, or bugs can also yield ideas for further improvements. Moreover, requests, initiatives, or ideas from the Sales and Research & Development (R&D) departments can be considered valuable sources as well.

3. Defining prioritization criteria

Prioritization starts with sorting the backlog. It is a highly strategic step that is fully based on data rather than a gut feeling. One key requirement for maintaining a healthy prioritization process is to create well-defined weights and evaluation criteria for backlog features.

Based on the nature of your product, you should define a set of evaluation criteria and use it to grade each backlog feature.

The next criteria can be incorporated and used for any product:

- **Revenues:** this criterion presents how much revenue the feature can likely generate. This is usually based on customers' or sales staff's feedback. Unless there is already an agreed-upon deal, the potential revenue will only be a guesstimate. Nevertheless, it remains a useful metric for prioritization as it enables the Product manager to avoid features with potentially low Return On Investment (ROI).
- **Market fit and market uniqueness:** market fit indicates if a certain feature resolves an existent problem for users. Market uniqueness measures how unique this new feature is in comparison to what competitors offer. These two metrics combined will highlight the most relevant features that have not yet been developed by the competition and thus makes a great opportunity for your product.
- **Complexity:** this criterion combines the overall complexity of executing and developing a feature. How many functions is this going to impact? What are the direct and potential hidden costs for each? You should aim for the shortest possible delivery time while maximizing the value that the feature can bring.

Other criteria you may consider include Risk and Cost.

Once you have identified and chosen your features' prioritization criteria, the next step is to give an estimate for each criterion. In traditional prioritization, you relatively compare all the items to each other using Fibonacci-inspired numbers (1, 2, 3, 5, 8, 13, 21,...). This means you give the smallest item a 1, the next smallest item a 2, etc. Make sure that you create enough spread within your range so you can really differentiate those criteria. Use 1 for really small items, and 21 should for really, really significant features.

Once you have estimated all of your features, you can easily compare which one must be given priority over the others. But, why take such rough estimates to prioritize tasks? Essentially all of your estimations are based on assumptions. It doesn't make sense to try to pin it down to detailed figures. You might have overlooked certain aspects, or failed to consider all of the factors involved. Making your estimations more precise creates the illusion that you have complete control over your backlog and prioritization, which you actually don't.

4. Maintaining the Backlog

It's important to keep in mind that your product backlog is a living document that is changing in priority often. After all, if you're following these steps, the top portion of your backlog should be disappearing after every sprint, as your team completes them. This means that some portion of the second-level items on the backlog will move up after every sprint as well, to the on-deck spot.

In order to efficiently maintain your backlog, feedback should be gathered. Stakeholders, customers, and support teams should be continually leveraged about new revelations and updates that may impact the product. Then, this feedback should be analyzed. It's the Product Owner's responsibility to lead these activities, commonly known as "backlog grooming" or "backlog refinement".

***

Prioritizing items on your product backlog has several advantages: You have clear reasons on why you are starting work on certain tasks first and you can share this with relevant stakeholders.

How long should a Sprint be?

Short Answer

Initially, sprint length always has to be between one to four weeks. Sprints length mainly depends on the project goal and duration: If the goal is risk reduction, then you should choose a shorter sprint length (1 week), if your goal is to develop a new product for which you already reduced basic risks, choose a medium sprint length (2 weeks), and if your goal is to develop or improve a product that is already profitable go for the longer sprint length (4 weeks).

Alternatively, projects shorter than six months should opt for 1-week sprints, projects that usually last about six to twelve months should go for 2-week sprints, and projects longer than one year should opt for 3 to 4-week sprints.

Explanation

A Sprint contains the four main Scrum events: Sprint Planning, Daily Scrum, Sprint Review, and Sprint Retrospective. The timebox of a sprint provides focus on things that are imminent and valuable with an aim to meet the sprint goal.

The Sprint functions as a closed feedback loop where impediments and issues in processes and practices are identified through regular inspection and adaptation. This enables the team's commitment to constant improvement and ensures the delivery of high-value products.

I am often asked, "How long should my team's Sprint be?" and "Does the Sprint have a fixed duration?" The answer is "It depends". Sprint length is not so cut and dry, as there are numerous factors that should contribute to your decision on whether to go for a long or a short sprint.

1. It depends

To make use of a sprint, you must be clear about the goal of your current project or project phases. If the goal is risk reduction, then you should choose a shorter sprint length. This is also true when you're not sure about what the customer wants or about how to best use new technology.

For early prototyping and business model validation, such as startups, most teams choose short sprints. This gives them plenty of checkpoints to correct the course, and these course corrections will be more drastic initially. Once basic validation and risk reduction happen, most teams switch to longer sprints, because course corrections will not be so drastic anymore and it's enough to do a reality check. When a product further stabilizes, some teams switch to the maximum length of a sprint length, as course corrections are even less drastic now, and conducting a review more often would not lead to additional course corrections.

How long your project runs can give you a clue towards your optimal sprint length as well. For instance, projects in an early prototyping or validation phase are seldomly longer than six months, more often they're two to three months long. And, having 4-week sprints in a short two months project would be almost like not being agile at all, as one checkpoint in the entire project won't help much.

On the other hand, projects for new products, for which basic risks have been reduced already, usually last about six to twelve months. For such a timespan, weekly checkpoints would be a little too much. You would most likely not adjust your course much after each sprint. So, many teams choose a medium sprint length. Moreover, if your project runs for significantly longer than one year (i.e. 2 or even 5 years), the same reasoning applies: Monthly checkpoints are enough and you wouldn't want to overwhelm your team with too many re-plannings, where in most cases not much would change.

When deciding on your sprint length, bear in mind that it shouldn't be changed after the sprint starts and that all of your sprints should be the same length. If you extend the sprint length, there would be a temptation to add more work which will not just impact the number of the user stories but will also make it difficult to get an accurate measure of your team's velocity.

This being said, having different sprint lengths for certain sprints to accommodate the holiday season, for instance, isn't actually a terrible idea. Involving the product owner and concerned stakeholders is important since a sprint is a feedback loop and their presence in the sprint review meeting is key in your Agile life cycle implementation.

In both situations, don't turn the sprint into a slog by forcing work to get "Done". When we rush things to get done, we sacrifice quality and invite chaos. A sprint isn't about 'busy work' or control over individual performance, which eventually leads to tyranny. You should use the sprint's increment to explore meaningful feedback that can help you better guide your product development process.

2. Short Sprint

"Make it two weeks" is the standard recommendation of most agile experts, and it's certainly a starting point with which you can hardly go wrong. So, if you're in a hurry or in doubt, a sprint length of two weeks will work for you. Why? Well, two weeks seems to be the most common sprint length in practice, it is kind of the middle between the possible extremes and it gives you enough benefits without the high cost. It's also easy enough for novice agile teams to understand and apply.

The Sprint length needs to be short enough so that the requirements churn is slower than the sprint length can accommodate. That is, if the Sprint is two weeks long, then the team is hoping that the changes in requirements happen less frequently than every two weeks. Meaning, stakeholders can expect to see their 'new stuff' done at the end of the sprint.

In today's environment, the requirements churn is typically too fast for the sprint: There are bugs to fix in systems, as well as emergencies to deal with within the company, and stakeholders are almost constantly changing their minds about what is important. All of these reasons contribute to the team's decision to shorten the sprint length or the planning cycle.

With a two-week sprint, more but shorter retrospectives are held by the team. The team has more opportunities to make adjustments, which allows them to improve their deliverables; frequent Sprint Reviews provide the Product Owner with more feedback, and therefore they have more opportunities to update their thoughts on the product backlog. This should largely eliminate the need for the Product Owner to ever ask for a change (e.g. new story) during an ongoing sprint.

Plus, impediments and slowdowns are identified more promptly since the team is expected to get features done by the end of every sprint. This pushes the team to come to terms with things that are holding them back. Shorter cycles also make planning easier, which increases focus and reduces ambiguity. The visibility of progress within a sprint improves when teams break features or stories into smaller chunks.

However, short sprints also involve some disadvantages. For instance, it's harder to get to a finished product at the end of a one or two-week cycle. Additionally, working in one-week sprints can be more stressful at first: people say that sprint meetings are too much overhead for a one-week sprint.

To conclude, if your goal is to develop a new product for which you already reduced basic risks, choose a medium sprint length of two weeks. The most common example is early product development, where you already validated basic assumptions, but you still need rapid feedback from your customers to sculpt the marketable product.

3. Long Sprint

It's a Scrum rule that a sprint should never last more than one month: If your sprint lasts more than one month, you are no longer using Scrum. It is easier to deliver a valuable chunk of work and have it marked as "Done" in one month rather than two weeks. Afterward, if your goal is to develop or improve a product that is already profitable (i.e. delivers value to customers in a proven way), go for the longer sprint length of one month.

In Sprint Planning, it is usually hard to plan adequately for a three to four-week sprint. This leads to more "dark work" being done, meaning new needs and features emerge more often mid-sprint. Thus, long sprints are more suitable when the work involved is more ambiguous and changes are less expected. With long sprints, the Product Owner will have fewer opportunities to improve the product. Consequently, fewer Sprint Retrospectives also lead to fewer explicit opportunities to improve as a team and a greater risk of sprint cancellation due to changes in the market or customer expectations.

***

The success of the Scrum team hinges on determining the right sprint length. Try to experiment with different sprint durations while taking into consideration factors contributing to the team's capacity to create "Done" increments. Once the right length is identified, keep it consistent to create a rhythm that will enable productivity and predictability.

Why use story points rather than hours for estimation in Scrum?

Short Answer

Story Points are a handy and efficient measurement technique for estimating the amount of effort a team needs to develop a particular feature. Using story points rather than hours for tasks estimates in Scrum helps you measure and track your team's velocity. Unlike hours, story points provide an accurate collaborative estimation of user stories.

Explanation

A Story Point is a unit of measurement used in the Scrum framework to estimate the difficulty of implementing a User Story. Story points take into consideration the amount of work to do, its complexity, and any risk or uncertainty involved in its execution.

Story Points proved to be a handy and efficient measurement technique for estimating the amount of effort a team needs to develop a particular feature. However, questions are always raised about estimates using story points: "Why points? Why not hours or days?" "I must do the planning, so do I need to convert points to a duration?" "Why this additional level of indirection?"

As a matter of fact, story points estimations have many advantages compared to estimates in hours or days, which we're explaining below.

1. Tracking velocity

Velocity is a metric for how much work a team can finish during one sprint and it's measured by summing up the total points of all fully completed user stories at the end of the sprint. Velocity is a great method for measuring and planning according to your team's capacity. For example, if a team can accomplish 50 points per sprint, it would be irrelevant to plan a new sprint involving 100 story points. Doing that will result in an uncompleted sprint and overwhelming frustration. Planning 50 to 60 points per sprint would be a more reasonable decision. If planned stories are completed before the end of the sprint, additional stories can be then added from the backlog.

With iterative development, the team is constantly learning about what they can do and how long it takes to do certain tasks. If estimates are in days, the team finds itself in the position of needing to frequently re-estimate stories based on current knowledge. This problem largely goes away with points: the fact that a team has learned to work twice as fast gets reflected in their velocity. And, as long as the story sizes are consistent between stories, no re-estimation is necessary.

2. Accuracy

Estimates are sometimes problematic taking into consideration that the person in charge of estimating a task isn't always the one who eventually implements it. Furthermore, estimation differences are frequent due to the variance in perspectives and experience. For instance, senior and junior developers may have different estimations of how many story points a task is worth. Using Story points, as an additional layer of estimation, are better than durations in bridging the gap between different assessments.

Estimates using actual hours or days require a lot of commitment, which can push the development team to either overestimate tasks or compromise quality in favor of speeding up execution. However, with story points, many team members find tasks estimation less intimidating and stressful since it doesn't directly involve durations.

Story points sequence

This being said, an approximative duration could be affected to story points in order to guide the team especially when they are new to the story points estimation technique.

When I worked for Foretheta, we used the Fibonacci sequence with the following estimations:

- **1 (XS; very small):** a straightforward issue that takes a few minutes or hours to accomplish. This is usually used for small bugs.
- **2 (S; small):** a task, with little complexity, that takes up to 1 day.
- **3 (M; medium):** tasks that need some research, but are still feasible in 1 to 3 days.
- **5 (L; large):** Tasks with high complexity that could take up to 3-5 days.
- **8 (XL; very large):** Tasks with a very high complexity that will require more than one week to complete. These issues usually require research or complex structure/coding. It's preferable to divide such tasks into smaller issues to improve tracking.
- **13 (XXL; extra-large):** Complexity here is extremely high. This is only used in rare cases where the task is completely ambiguous and there is no clear way on how it should be divided. The task should be split into smaller tasks at a later time when the team gains more knowledge.

***

Story Points have earned the reputation of being a reliable metric that's independent of the skill or experience of team members, allowing you to assess the velocity of your team and plan your project releases. Some specialists prefer combining both story points and man-hours. But still, story points offer the greatest utility for high-level planning.

How do you define a project delivery date in Agile?

Short Answer

Predictable delivery is usually what business stakeholders seek. To estimate the delivery date of your project start with estimating the Product backlog. This backlog can be recorded as epics, stories, or tasks. Next, determine your Sprint length and calculate your team's velocity. You will be able to do that with enough data from previous projects. Finally, calculate the number of required iterations to determine an estimation for your project delivery date.

Explanation

Even though the scope is variable in Agile, stakeholders still ask how long it will take to complete part or all of the project work. A predictable delivery date is generally what stakeholders look for in order to make strategic decisions based on their priorities.

Clients could have different strategies. For some, it is more important to launch their products or features on a fixed date, others opt to only launch when a particular capability is available. Without being able to estimate delivery dates, business decisions can become difficult to make and stakeholders might feel frustrated with the process.

1. Estimating the product backlog

Your backlog should define your initial product vision, be that a prototype, MVP, full product backlog, etc. When estimating tasks, you should opt for story points rather than hours, days, or t-shirt sizes. Story Points provide relative values of the required level of effort, taking into account the amount of work that must be accomplished, the risk and uncertainty brought by the item, and the complexity of the task.

In order to accurately assign story points for your backlog items, you should involve your team in the process. You can rely on different methods to collectively estimate your product backlog items.

Planning poker, for instance, is a card-based technique and it's one of the most popular estimation methods. Team members discuss the feature, asking the

Product Owner questions when needed. Then, privately, each team member picks out one card that indicates their estimate. All cards should be then revealed at once. If all team members select the same value, it gets defined as the estimate. Otherwise, a discussion of the different opinions and estimates will take place before re-estimating again.

2. Determining the velocity of your team

Along with estimating your product backlog, you need to also determine your team's velocity to be able to estimate a delivery date. A team's velocity indicates the average number of story points delivered per sprint. Velocity is measured by calculating the total points of all the fully completed user stories. Please note that partially done tasks should not be counted.

For example, in a given sprint, if your team completes four tasks with story points 3, 5, 8, and 2 respectively as well as half of a 13-story-points-worth task, the velocity of your team is 18 (3+5+8+2).

Enough data from previous projects can help you ascertain your completion date. For forecasting purposes, ideally, the average of the last three Sprints' Velocity should be used. Of course, this means it takes at least three sprints for a team to determine its velocity more accurately.

Typically, a team needs several sprints of working as a unit to produce enough data for a predictable, reliable velocity. But, new teams that haven't finished a sprint together yet don't have this data. In this case, the best way to determine the team's velocity is to simply make an educated guess. For the first sprint, have the team plan until they feel like they have a workload that they're comfortable with and confident that they can finish by the end of the sprint.

3. Calculating the project delivery date

Once you have estimated your product backlog and determined your team's velocity, you can now calculate your project's potential delivery date. For instance, if your team has a sprint velocity of 50 story points and the required features are estimated at 150 story points, the client should be informed that three sprints are required to accomplish the defined scope requirements. Keep in mind that this is just an estimation and not a commitment.

Contractually, when sending a Statement of Work to a client for an Agile project I usually emphasize that the scope of the project will vary depending on the changing requirements and understanding of the project. Hence, it's recommended to define the project cost based on man-hour rates rather than a fixed price. For example, if your development team is composed of 4 members with an hourly rate of $75 each, an iteration of two weeks would cost $21,000 ($75 x 4 members x 7h x 10 days).

***

Bear in mind that there are some caveats to this form of estimating. Firstly, estimating a project based on data from previous projects might be very risky when there can be and usually are, many differences between projects. But, if you decide to do it, you'll need at least some consistency between the teams of both projects. That shouldn't be a problem for most established cross-functional teams. However, if you're going to try to extrapolate a completion rate for a small team of say 2 people, using data from a project which had 6 people then obviously you have to normalize your data and hope that normalization doesn't skew it too much, which it probably will.

Secondly, estimating delivery dates, especially if the backlog is large-sized, can be subject to a great deal of uncertainty because a backlog is by its nature speculative. The more you try to estimate the less likely you're going to be accurate with that estimate. I would always advocate stripping the backlog back to the barest MVP and only attempt to estimate that at the most.

Get your **IT Project Management course** along with the full set of 20+ Professional Templates & checklists for FREE through this link: https://bit.ly/BonusCourse

To enroll, click on "Take the course", sign up, and start learning!

Feel free to get in touch at **hello@yassinetounsi.com** in case you have any inquiries or face any issues with the course.

Did you find this guide helpful? If so, I'd love to hear about it. Honest reviews help other readers find the right book for their needs.

About the Author

Yassine is a PMP® certified Instructor & Author with more than 10 years of experience in the IT field, moving up in his career through multiple positions like a Business Developer, Account manager, Functional consultant, Product owner, Office manager, up to being currently a Project manager.

Managing and leading both on-site and remote projects, in the public and private sectors, Yassine is passionate about helping and sharing his Project Management expertise and knowledge.

Relying on his academic background along with his real-life experience managing projects in Telecommunications, Retail, Financial Services, and more, Yassine aims to present practical rich content suitable for beginners as well as professionals in the PM field.

Yassine strongly believes in the practical methodology, offering easy to apply knowledge that he is certain about its efficiency considering that he practices what he preaches in his daily position as a Project Manager.

Printed in Great Britain
by Amazon